SEASONED WITH SALT

. SEASONED
WITH
SALT .

Mary Travis Arny

Philadelphia

THE WESTMINSTER PRESS

Library of Congress Catalog Card No.: 54-9399

PRINTED IN THE UNITED STATES OF AMERICA

Author's Note, Preface, and Dedication

THIS is the story of a house and of those who have lived, laughed, and loved in it. The characters, saints and otherwise, are all real, except for Mr. Hector Slaight. In his case the things he did happened, but not, thank heaven, all at once. Mr. Slaight never was, so don't try to place him.

As to the title, Polly found it, and in the oddest way. She insists that I told it to her in the middle of the night, which I most certainly did not. I never heard it in all my life, and I am certain that she at the age of seven had not read the book of Leviticus either! Nevertheless she came down with it one fine morning, and here it is. So, to whatever benign ghost was up to helping us out, we are grateful. Usually our ghosts are sneezing, slamming doors, or hiding things where we can't find them.

The verse is an unfamiliar one, found in Leviticus 2:13. " And every oblation of thy meat offering shalt thou season with salt; neither shalt thou suffer the salt of the covenant of thy God to be lacking."

Since the foundation upon which our family rests is an unswerving belief that life was meant to be savored and enjoyed, and that it is not at all necessary to be dull in order to achieve decency, the phrase has stuck.

So, therefore, with love and affection this book is dedicated to all those who during two hundred years have partaken of bread and salt, love and laughter, life and adventure, at Tongueslip, and most of all to Robert.

MARY ARNY.

SEASONED WITH SALT

[1]

IN 1916 it simply wasn't done for an American clergyman to go to war, which was probably one of the reasons Dad did it. Our family is not known for the calmness with which it appraises any situation. We could never, by the wildest stretch of the imagination, be accused of being lukewarm about anything. Dad was furious about the *Lusitania* and deeply shocked by the execution of Edith Cavell. Seeing things from a slightly different viewpoint is our forte, and while the rest of the clergy were tearfully trying to justify the text about the other cheek, Dad insisted on pointing out the one in Luke that is carefully overlooked by the cloth in general: " He that hath no sword, let him sell his garment and buy one " (Luke 22:36).

There were a lot of people in the parish who objected violently. There always are. That is the beauty of a parish, it is never dull ! Some of them left the church, but there were more who took a fierce pride in their sandy-haired fighting parson, as he came to be known throughout the land. He was small in stature really, but people describing him always say he was tall and strong. I think he was meant to be; but he never got enough to eat as a child.

Of course you can't run a big house on the wages of a buck tommy in the British Expeditionary Force, and so we had to sell our home.

Mother and I moved into rooms on the second floor of the last remaining "Dames School." This had its advantages in that, at a tender age, I was well indoctrinated with manners and propriety, an education that I undoubtedly needed but did not enjoy at all.

When Dad was gassed at Vimy Ridge and invalided home, my private rejoicing lay in the fact that I would once again have an ally in the battle for corduroy knickers and a turtle-neck sweater as opposed to Liberty silks and featherstitched flannel petticoats.

The knickers had to wait, however, until we could find a house of our own. Miss Edythe and Miss Helen would not tolerate them. It was definitely out of order to have trousers of any kind in close proximity to their daily living, and only the fact that Dad's were respectable black broadcloth, tailored by Brooks' Brothers clerical tailors, made it possible for them to endure his. He was always exceedingly well groomed in the pulpit. Elsewhere he did as he pleased in the matter of sartorial elegance.

Dad admired and respected these proper virgins, but he found it a constant trial to censor every sentence before he uttered it. The result was that dinner conversation deteriorated into a series of "Yes, ma'am's" and "No, ma'am's" which we all knew he could not endure for long.

Next door to the church was an enormous Victorian mansion, no longer inhabited by its owner, Miss Lottie. Replete with gingerbread scrollwork, wrought-iron thistles, and a sagging port-cochere, it was reminiscent of an elegant but somewhat inebriated Astor who had been chucked unceremoniously off her plush horse.

It was redeemed by lilacs, which poked their fragrant blossoms through the shattered second-story windows, an enormous garden in which the birds sang uninterrupted by human presence, and a tall pine tree which shaded it against the summer sun and filled the air with balm.

Mother stood outside the church on Sunday and chanced to remark: "What a lot one could do with that old house! It has inherent charm."

Hence Tongueslip!

Dad called on Miss Lottie that very afternoon, and bought the house, cash on the barrelhead.

If you saw Helen Hayes in *Victoria Regina*, you have seen Miss Lottie. At the time she was living in an apartment uptown, and Tongueslip was theoretically rented to a family of Boers who might well have been the inspiration for the use of that noun as a term of contempt.

They had folded their bank account, and it was the only thing they had folded, and departed silently, leaving Miss Lottie unrecompensed for many a long month's rent. When we went into the house for the first time I thought that my mother, my impregnable mother, would weep. But it was not for nothing that she is known as the Duchess. She behaved accordingly.

All the accumulated rubbish of their three years' unpaid tenancy was thrown into the butler's pantry, and the stench was overpowering. The lovely little conservatory was a mass of ragweed, stinkweed, and bindweed.

The mustard-colored tiles were falling out of the fireplaces and the floors were a sticky black which made a sound like flypaper when we walked on them.

Miss Lottie retained her composure and went to the telephone, only to discover that it too had been removed for lack of payment.

We retired to the church office, whence we hired three men with scrubbing brushes, one man with a shovel, a horse, and a wagon. It took them six full working days to remove the dirt and debris sufficiently to enable us to begin helping Miss Lottie to recognize her personal possessions.

Miss Lottie's composure began to break, and the Duchess put her hand on the old lady's arm. Miss Lottie shook her

11

head slowly. "My dear, you mustn't feel sorry for me. I do love the old house, and I dislike seeing it looking so ill. For us it has served its purpose. My mother brought up her family here, and I brought up mine. We are all as old and worn out as the house seems. It can be fixed, but we can not. It is time for the old place to have a new, young family to be happy in it. That is what will make it well again."

The Duchess took her at her word and smiled. The battered remnants went out the faster and were piled at the curb. There they attracted the notice of a secondhand dealer, who promptly pushed the doorbell. The Duchess let him in.

I was too young to classify him as to race, but I do remember that his clothes were greasy, his nails black, and his eyes reminded me of those of a fish too long held on ice. He went through the house with Miss Lottie, making offers for the various pieces of furniture. For a horrible Empire sideboard, lacking three of its four pineapples, he offered fifty dollars; for a table with a cracked marble top, twenty-five; for the battered horsehair sofa, thirty; for the mahogany Governor Winthrop desk, seventy; and for a charming curly maple table, thirty. His prices for the derelicts were so high that Miss Lottie's face beamed, and she was willing to overlook the pitifully inadequate bids on the real treasures.

The deal was completed. The dealer reached into his grimy pocket and pulled out a wad of bills. "I haven't a big truck with me, Mrs. So I'll just pay for the desk and table, take them along, and come back for the rest tomorrow."

The Duchess gave him one long and penetrating look. "You will get out that door before I count ten." Ice seemed to form in the windows. Miss Lottie was aghast. She saw her golden fortune vanishing in the frost. The dealer protested that the deal had been made, and that it was none of the Duchess' business.

Miss Lottie started to agree, and was almost rude to Mother. Mother stood firm and the dealer departed.

12

Miss Lottie turned from the slamming door with white lips. "Whatever do you *mean* by interfering? He would have paid me three times as much for the old things as I can get anywhere else."

Mother shook her head. "Miss Lottie, I will give you twice what he offered for the table and desk. He would have taken the choice things for a song, and you would never have seen him again."

The Duchess made her promise good, and much of this tale is being written on the mahogany Winthrop. The dealer succeeded in his skulduggery in another home that very day. When Miss Lottie heard of it, her fingers moved lovingly over the fine old pieces which had been saved from a fate worse than death and told us, as only those who are very old can tell, with minute detail, remembered from a childhood when warmth and love abounded, the story of every stick and stone in Tongueslip; that is, all of the story she knew.

"It was stone when we bought it, and not very fashionable. It was so very plain, so very simple. When Harry came back from the War Between the States he wanted to remodel it and bring it up to date. So we added a wing, put on the verandas and covered the pine floors with parquet. We put in the Baltimore heaters and closed up those dreadful old-fashioned fireplaces, and replaced the pine paneling with golden oak. We got the iron thistles on the roof from Scotland, and my mother used to love the way the fir trees whispered against them, as though they remembered the same things from the old country. Mother brought the firs in her satchel when she came so as to have part of Scotland with her. She brought the ivy on the west wall too. She'd taken a cutting from Edinburgh Castle.

"On the east wall she planted ivy from Mount Vernon. My mother loved green growing things. The first thing she did after she had returned her calls was to form a club, and to plant trees along all the streets in town.

" She and her friends planted the elms and the maples along the avenue, and you can see from their size that it was a long time ago."

I looked at the old swamp maple that six of us children could not embrace, and understood " a long time ago" for the first time.

We could see that she was tired, so the Duchess went to the kitchen to make a cup of tea.

I remember how the barrels which held potatoes and sugar and tea and coffee beans fascinated me then. Although they were not filled at the moment, it required little imagination to know how delectable they would smell when they were, and it was a constant enchantment to swing them out on their pivots, lift the wooden lids, and shout into the hollow darkness to hear the sepulchral echo of the veriest inanity.

I carried in the tray, with the Lowestoft tea set, pot in a straw cozy, pound cake decorated with crisp toasted almonds, and slices of bread and butter so thin as to seem transparent. The Duchess led the old lady on and on through the eternal ramblings of a weary memory stirred by interest again, long after all other listeners had become bored with what seemed to them unending repetitions. Miss Lottie's memory of the present was blurred, but we were able to recover much of what had happened long ago.

We spent days together at Tongueslip, helping her to sort her things and get our things settled, and finally the day came when the deed changed hands.

I remember how steady her fingers were when she signed it, and how my father's strong lean hand dipped a goose-quill pen for her, because she liked quills better and stanchly maintained that stub pens were for savages, and I remember how the old lady read out in her firm, soft voice, "In consideration of one dollar, love, and affection, I, Lottie Littlejohn, hereby transfer to Thomas and Mary Travis, their heirs and assigns forever . . ." (You won't mind, dear sir, if we do not mention

14

the sum, I'd like it to read that way, it always has.)

"In consideration of one dollar, love, and affection" — **of** all covenants the most binding.

I HAVE always been glad that Miss Lottie was unequal to a descent into the cellar, for Dad was almost unequal to the ascent after he saw it!

The stairs were so narrow and had so little head room that one felt certain that only a hunchbacked dwarf could possibly have tended the furnace. It was impossible to stand upright in any portion of that cellar. One supposes that Captain Harry had adequate service and never felt called upon to investigate conditions belowstairs. It must have been a backbreaking task to fire the boiler. It stood in a pit, surrounded by ashes, and leered.

I remember that furnace with horror and nightmares. It looked like an Artzybasheff drawing from the cover of *Time*. Pipes writhed out in every direction, and its eyes and mouth flamed like the hotbox of Shadrach, Meshach, and Abednego. There was a reason why the pipes twisted. It was impossible for them to go straight. The walls were three feet thick, hand-hewn stone, and pointed up with clay.

Mother, being only a scant five feet in height, and very slender, was able to negotiate the paths left by a procession of incredibly untidy furnace men and to survey the situation with what remnants of serenity she could muster. "Nothing," she decided, "has gone out of this house but the dead, since the beginning of recorded time."

The erstwhile tenants must have subsisted largely upon eggs, for every corner not occupied by ashes was crammed

15

with empty egg boxes. It is inconceivable that anyone could ever have eaten the contents of those ubiquitous boxes, but the evidence was there and not to be denied.

The man with the shovel, the horse, and the wagon was again recalled. He worked for days and finally got the cellar clear enough to reveal the hard dirt floor and the huge timbers which had been so veiled in cobwebs as to be completely invisible.

The Duchess poked and prodded. She rediscovered the random pine flooring which had been covered during the remodeling by Captain Harry and Miss Lottie. When she saw the width of the boards, a glint came into her eyes that boded no good for the already sadly depleted family exchequer.

She extracted hand-wrought nails from the uprights and haunted museums trying to find their counterparts. She made rubbings of H and L hinges and tracings of iron latches. She went to the hall of records in Newark and lifted tome after tome of deeds from the dusty archives. She became thoroughly conversant with the family histories of the respected Ketchums, Jacobuses, Van Ripers, Garrabrandts, and Speers.

She even knew what color the VanderZees' cow was, since one of the landmarks commonly appearing was the boulder to which Elizabeth VanderZee's red heifer was tethered.

There is an enormous glacial boulder in front of our church, now worn smooth by generations of pants seats sliding down it, which may perhaps be that so important stone. There were other stones of different shape and cast which she scrubbed clear of moss in order to decipher names and dates, but this activity was somewhat disrupted by the fact that outdoor fireplaces were beginning to come into fashion and the overgrown graveyard in Bloomfield had yielded up many a marker for this quite practical use. The Duchess got quite royally scratched by brambles in the process of her investigations, and read the hearthstones of a good many barbecues but eventually she came up triumphant with the answer.

"Tongueslip," she told us, "was built by one Christian Interest, a cobbler, husband of Fruitchy Interest, in the year 1754. He owned several pieces of property in the vicinity and prospered well, since when Washington's rabble in arms came pounding south from Hackensack, apparently defeated and desolate, Christian was the only cobbler in the area, and he plied a good trade fixing the ragged boots of an army in despair. Washington had headquarters in the old Crane mansion, and must have ridden down Watchung Avenue, then Oak Tree Lane, on many occasions. The Algonquin Indians traded and hunted over this area too. It's alive with history."

At the time I wasn't much impressed with the data of this kind, but be it known for the record that nothing but the dinner conversations at Tongueslip really contributed to my college degrees. I passed American history only by the grace of God, and a thorough knowledge of Washington's New Jersey campaigns. An intimate acquaintance with the Leni-Lenape, Delaware, or Algonquin Indians, enabled me to write at such length on New Jerseyana that I am certain the professor never finished reading the paper, and gave my blue book a grade of "one" out of sheer astonishment at the volume of my information, which may or may not have outweighed the accuracy.

The Duchess' interest was of a more complicated nature. She was determined to take Tongueslip apart and put it back together again. She wanted to see what it had looked like to General Washington, Father of His Country, and to Christian Interest, cobbler to the Army.

Incidentally, just as an aside, Nathan Hale was executed just a few days before Washington came to this area. Statues and pictures show him with a rope around his neck, but there seems to be considerable evidence that he was shot.

Dad argued about that, and about the remodeling of the house. He was adamant. He had lived in trenches, shivered in mud and dugouts, been exposed to the elements, as much as he cared to be. He had a roof over his head and he intended to keep it there, interest Christian or not.

For a while he did so. But when he discovered that thirty tons of coal kept the north end of the house at a perilous 32½ and the south end at 212 Fahrenheit; that every rain had to be met with dishpans on the stairs and buckets in the bedrooms; that the pipes spilled more water down the hand-hewn oak beams than into the bathtubs; he told Mother to go ahead and remodel it. The only stipulation was that it must be finished before church opened in the fall. He himself retired to Canada with a camera and a fishing rod.

The architects were summoned to a conclave. The historians were consulted. Every expert in the parish contributed his or her bit of special and valuable knowledge. " Uncle " George Holmes knew the history of the town from beginning to end. Mr. Dilts was an authority on early lighting fixtures. Mr. DeGolyer knew early American libraries from one end to the other. Mr. Douglass Fitch, the architect, had a sixth sense for what good craftsmanship must have been in the period.

Mr. Mitchell knew all the ins and outs of paint; others were up on early papers, and woods. Such a gathering of people about to have a field day with their hobbies has seldom been seen, and the Duchess had a field day of her own, that is, until the actual face-lifting began!

Little by little the gingerbread came off. Little by little the old house emerged. As the Victorian excrescences disappeared, the shape and form of Christian's original home became apparent. It had been a large single-roomed dwelling, with a sleeping loft. The house had been built of field stone on the west wall, and cut sandstone on the other three sides. As he had prospered, additions had been made, each clearly defined by the difference in the technique of stonecutting. It looked as though restoration to the original lines would be fairly simple.

We had reckoned without the Civil War. After that tragic

18

episode men had believed that war would never again come to our country. They had decided that it was sound economics to build for eternity, and they had put up their additions and corrections accordingly!

They put things together to stay! The nails they used were six inches long, the beams they used were solid oak, the clapboards they lapped were two inches thick, and wrecking bars often slipped when pried against them. It became my task to maintain a first-aid station for the workmen. Strict orders were given that any scratch, however slight, was to have immediate attention. Only one man disregarded these instructions, and he ended up with a case of blood poisoning that laid him up for weeks and nearly cost him his right arm.

I remember Big Ben, the boss carpenter, particularly. He was more concerned by the pollution of my small ears with the blasphemies occasioned by saws and chisels dulled on oak, stone, and old nails than he was about the scratches I tended. As I look back on it now, I am grateful that I heard those lusty workmen. They inured me to shock from the comparative lily-whiteness that passes for obscenity in the cocktail congregations, and among adolescents who, priding themselves on the swiftness with which they are going to the dogs, betray by their completely inadequate vocabularies the happy fact that they do not even know where the dogs are.

The roof was successfully raised three feet so that the third floor would be habitable. Captain Harry must have had Blackamoors there as well as in the cellar. We had to crawl the long corridor to the water storage tanks! The dormers on the side walls, east and west, had to come off in order to achieve the lifting. For weeks we lived in a sort of palatial lean-to, with no windows and no doors. The electricity, gas, and hot water were cut off to avoid the dangers of fire and flood, and Mother and I used the facilities at the parish house next door for everything that necessity entailed.

It was during this trying period that I began to have a

glimmer of Chloe's true worth. Always pleasant, where others would have grumbled, she managed faultless popovers in the midst of chaos. I do believe that the ability to present a pleasing meal must come high on the list of cardinal virtues. For as I think back over my life I am convinced that much of life's woe and bitterness comes from quick tempers produced by rumbling tummies.

Tongueslip was a mess — a mess such as I have seen only once since that reconstruction era. That was on the day after the 1938 hurricane, when, because of death of a dearly beloved friend, we drove to Orient Point on the extreme eastern tip of Long Island.

There, among schooners tossed up in the streets, stood Tongueslip's counterpart, with the entire front wall ripped off and leaning dizzily. In the attic, where it had long ago been placed for eventual grandchildren, stood a white rocking horse with its mane flying in the still tumultuous wind, and on the front porch was a box of eggs (curiosity prompted me to examine it) which, with the house torn down about it, the storm of the century still howling, and the salt waves lapping a few feet away, somehow remained miraculously unbroken.

The Duchess was like those eggs. How she ever survived that summer only God Almighty can explain. It was terrific! Mosquitoes made sleep impossible, yet we could not leave the house unguarded and open to any prowler who cared to loot it. We stuck it through.

When the workmen got the side walls back on again, things were better. Of course there were no windows, but not quite so many June bugs sputtered in the candle flames, and the mosquitoes were evidently satiated with Travis blood and had gone elsewhere. Lem, our faithful setter, relaxed a little, and did not prowl the halls in search of intruders all night, and his soft white fur under my hand was a comfort.

No doubt by now Dad has been consigned to the doghouse as a welsher, but in all fairness it must be admitted that he had no idea of the extent to which the work would go, and he did have to go fishing because a large part of our income at that time came from his lectures to sportsmen's clubs. He pioneered the sixteen millimeter motion pictures of animals in their native haunts, *The Wilderness Dwellers*, which Mr. Disney has now so superbly perfected, and I can even remember the days when we had caviar every night for dinner. Somebody had particularly enjoyed a trip Dad had sent him on and expressed his appreciation by having a case of delicacies from his importing house delivered to us each week.

The outside work on stone and stucco was completed. The painting began. McDermott, the Scottish painter, abominated the plantings around the house which Mother had fought to preserve. He slammed his ladders down on the bulbs and the lilacs and muttered imprecations through his walrus mustache.

Futher evidence of Chloe's wisdom! She made tea and shortbread and the Duchess invited McDermott in for a " cuppa." He sat on the edge of the chair at first, but gradually he relaxed and crossed his legs, and a glow of friendly contentment came over him. I would have sworn he was in kilts with a bagpipe beside him, and somehow Edinburgh Castle sneaked into the conversation. The story of the ivy and how it had been brought to Tongueslip by a lonely lassie who wanted a bit of auld lang syne drifted across the odor of shortbread and tea, and when McDermott went back out, the burring edict went forth: " Na drappe paint on that ivy, lads. It's fra *the* castle," and the plantings at Tongueslip survived. For years I thought that Edinburgh Castle was the only one in the world. I daresay McDermott still thinks so. In any case he sent me a sumptuous pillow with the stately old pile embroidered on it for a wedding present.

Now all that remained was the interior finishing and the plumbing. We ripped tons of golden oak curlicues, and gilded statues, which adorned every newel post, from the interior. They went the way of the Boer's debris, together with the mustard-colored tiles and Baltimore heaters from the chimney breasts. It was at this point that the only serious calamity of the summer occurred.

The mason was a surly brute, determined on his own way. He knew all the answers, and for the record he knew them all wrong, as such people are apt to do. He made a miserable botch of matching the outside stucco — it still is several shades off — and while everybody else labored lovingly and overtime to help the Duchess to meet her deadline, he dallied over the fish pool, in which he left the drain end under three feet of concrete and did not mark it on the blueprints.

When he came to the chimneys, he was armed with a cold chisel and a sledge hammer. His biceps were as thick as his head and he caught the plaster breast a terrific clip. We heard the sound of stone and the Duchess reached to catch his hand. He wrenched away and socked again. The cold steel caught on the face of the underlying chimney face and ripped a piece of stone the size of my hand from the single slab which constitutes the top piece.

Mr. Fitch sent him to work in the cellar while he and Mother and I gently picked the plaster and tiles off the fireplace. There he took his revenge by deepening the floor three feet and doing such a putrid job of setting the brick that it leaks like a sieve in every rain. Christian's work is still, after two centuries, dry as a bone. That fellow's leaves us with a muddy swimming pool each and every spring. Since there is no drain, we have to carry the water out in buckets, which, when you consider the amount of liquid contained in a cellar thirty feet wide and a hundred feet long, not to mention the water's being eight to fifteen inches deep, is a sorry task indeed.

Not content with that, he laid all the flagstones without tamping or cinders, and the sidewalks and terraces all had to be reset the next year.

The other workmen made up for it! The Duchess has a soft spot in her heart for young men who build and make and fix.

22

She understands them and respects their skill. They love her and will turn themselves inside out to see that she gets perfection. They worked overtime, they hired extra hands, they went " out straight " to see that her contract with Dad was met and that Tongueslip should be habitable before church opened.

The last item, we thought, was the furnace. The Duchess wanted the boiler put in the center of the house, but the experts assured her that it would not thus provide adequate heat. They were in fact so sure of their computations that they said they would guarantee the job only if she let them put it in the north cellar. She bowed to the inevitable. An early frost was their undoing!

The south end sizzled when the north end touched seventy. They moved the boiler to the south end. The north end froze solid and the pipes split.

They had guaranteed a job, and they were gentlemen. They put in two boilers, and they are there to this day.

Dad returned to Tongueslip and saw the bills. He was livid. The only thing he could ever do in such a state was to take immediate action. The only action left to take was to fire the laborers who were cleaning up the mess of wood and shingles in the yard.

" Why on earth are you burning that stuff? It should be piled neatly and we can use it in the fireplaces. It will save hundreds of dollars in fuel these next winters."

The workmen disappeared. Mother said nothing. Dad worked all day Monday stacking wood. On Tuesday he labored grimly. On Wednesday he went often to the store for tobacco. On Thursday we found him feeding a roaring bonfire which caused our back door neighbor Mr. Slaight to complain bitterly to the police.

In order to avoid Mr. Slaight's onslaught Dad retired to the library, which at that point was still in the front of the house. Its walls were lined with formal stacks and on the end of each was a hunting or fishing trophy of some sort. I remember a moose head, some caribou antlers, a tremendous alligator skin, and a tarpon. On the top shelf was a plaster statue of two cherubs reading a book.

Most of the children of the neighborhood, then as now, haunted Tongueslip. Robert Arny and his younger brother Malcolm were examining the moose. Dad took them on a guided tour, showed them his stuffed birds, his butterflies, and his mineral collection, explaining carefully just how, when, and why each prize had been taken. What the story lacked in accuracy it gained in interest and the Arny brothers were enraptured, but Dad learned a sad lesson that day. When they came to the cherubs, Malcolm looked at them wide-eyed.

"Dr. Travis, where did you shoot the babies?"

Poor Dad! He came to dinner in a state of deep distress. "Mary," he said to the Duchess, "do I give the impression of being a man who is capable of stuffing infants for decorative purposes?"

Mother threw back her head and laughed. "Not very often, dear, only when I fail to follow the precepts of Mr. Micawber."

"Well, that being the case, I'll leave them." He shook his head, puzzled.

I don't know where the cherubs went eventually. I have not seen them for years; neither can I find the cast-iron thistles which Miss Lottie loved so. The moose head is back in Maine, where Rupert and Ross Hughes had to take the side off their house to get it in, and the alligator skin has gone to dust, but Tongueslip still has its trophies of a different kind.

[3]

IT WAS shortly before the house was finished that Mother's sister became blind. Tante Bess and Uncle John had always lived in Montclair, but when it became apparent that she would never see again, they moved to the city, where life could be lived on one level and where Uncle John could be with her more on account of the time saved from commuting.

Mother's brother, Howard, had always lived with Tante Bess, but he wanted to stay in the country, and since we had room and to spare, it was arranged that he should live with us. His arrival heralded a new era at Tongueslip.

Unkie was a sociable soul, a catalyst. He had sat in the New York Assembly, been the religious reporter on the *World*, and was at the time in Wall Street. He played a brilliant game of bridge, kept right along with the Duchess — who was a Metropolitan star — at golf, and spent a good deal of his time on yachts and at country clubs.

So far as I was concerned he was a most welcome addition to the family circle because he was a whiz at math and Latin. He loved to help me with my lessons and was a born teacher. He would sit with his pipe clenched between his teeth, one of which was very sharp and drilled a neat hole in the stem, and repeat patiently, " Mary, I can teach you Latin, but I cannot learn it for you."

He helped me with Caesar's *Gallic Wars*, not so much by dinning declensions and conjugations into my head as by making me hear the tramp of the legions across Gaul, and see Ariovistus with his armor and his broadsword so realistically that I felt I had an ally directly behind me when I faced Miss Dwyer, who was really an excellent teacher but nevertheless struck terror to my heart by her scathing, " *Miserabile dictu, non paratus.*"

Until I had sat with Unkie, I did not realize that history was real and alive, that pons asinorum was a miraculous feat of skill, that x's and figures were as infinite in scope and imagination as the beloved novels of Jules Verne. On the more practical side he paid me fifty dollars a year for keeping my room in order!

It was not until a good many years later that I realized that during all the time he was with us he was seriously ill. No one would ever have guessed it from his manner or his behavior.

To us in our era of X-ray and fluoroscope, it is inconceivable that the cause of his pain should have been unfathomable to the medical profession, but it is a fact that common use of the X-ray and fluoroscope is comparatively recent.

It began in the oddest sort of way. Unkie was sailing to Havana with his Amherst roommate, Arthur James, aboard the *Coronet*. During his absence, Grandmother Wilson, whom I do not remember, woke suddenly to see him standing at the foot of her bed, blood dripping from a wound in his head and soaking through the bandages. She asked him what on earth had happened, but he only shook his head and disappeared.

Grandmother was beside herself. My other uncle, James, had died of yellow fever in Rio because someone had forgotten to meet him and left him in the unscreened city. She called the family and told them what had happened. Like most families with a good deal of common sense, they pooh-poohed her, and assured her that it was just a dream.

Imagine their feelings when Unkie returned, and had no sooner gotten through the door of the house than Grandmother sat him down and asked, " Howard, did anything happen to you on September 14? "

He hesitated a minute and then laughed: " Well, as a matter of fact, yes. One of the men forgot to tie the boom. It swung over and struck me on the head. They fished me out of the sharks, unconscious. But how did you know? "

Grandmother didn't know how she knew. Nobody did, and it is highly probable that nobody ever will. Things like that do happen, and with enough regularity in our family so that we are inclined to pay some attention to them. We do not explain them. We stay as far away from them as possible. Often it is wiser and pleasanter not to be too farsighted.

In any case the true extent of the injury was not discovered for years — in fact, not until after Unkie's death, when Dr. John Erdman commented that the fracture, which extended across the top of his head from ear to ear, had caused such pressure on his brain that it was nothing short of a miracle that he had not gone raving mad.

I assure you that I have never known anyone more completely rational. The only trouble was that at times he completely forgot who he was and where he was, and would disappear for weeks on end. Fortunately he always gravitated to the same circle, the University Club in whatever place he happened to be when amnesia overtook him, and so he never came to any serious harm.

In appearance he was round, a series of warming circles: round head; round horn-rimmed glasses; round of body without being fat, which was in itself a minor miracle, for he loved good food — not cakes and pies and candies, but strange things which made every meal an adventure.

He would stop at the Washington Market, where he knew all the mongers and they him, and he would bring home mysterious packages wrapped in heavy oiled paper and carried with a round wooden handle hooked into the string: guinea hens, enormous shrimp, buffalo steak once, swordfish which was then a novelty; papayas, Turkish coffee, cheeses, jasmine tea, beaver tails, truffles, lobster, and endive. He would show Chloe how to prepare them with piquant sauces and dressings, and praise her skill with words as perfect and as well-chosen as her condiments.

27

I cannot remember or describe his clothes. He was one of those geniuses who is so perfectly tailored as to belong to no period in the history of costume, and his voice was as cosmopolitan as his dress.

It is a strange thing how the voice is so living that it is the first thing to escape memory when it is gone. The same thing is true of bird songs, and surf, and the wind, and running brooks. One knows that one was moved by their music, but the mind cannot recapture the cadence until somewhere, suddenly, it is heard again and recognized.

It was Unkie who loved the garden at Tongueslip most. He would catch the first train from the city after the exchange closed, get into his working clothes, and go to it. He grew squash without borers, blanched celery, and created a miracle of green growing things, than which nothing ever tasted any better. Only one plant defied his efforts — lettuce. That he could not grow, and I could. I never told him that when I cleaned the rabbit cages I buried the straw in my small plot of garden. That may or may not have been the secret. In any case my lettuce was out of this world!

I would give much to be able to sit around the hearth at Tongueslip and hear again such talk as we had in those days. Dad, Unkie, Mr. DeGolyer, Dr. Fosdick, Mr. Cox; Hugh Black and Alexander Black — not kin except in mind and heart, but brothers in a world of interest; Judge Porter, Hans Folkers, Dr. Holland, and all those who had the world, and great dreams of its future, at their finger tips. There were giants in the earth in those days, and they opened long vistas to a small child, allowed to sit until bedtime and listen, and courteously attended when she dared to chime in. That was the miracle, I suppose; they treated me with grave courtesy though I was only ten. That is the miracle that distinguishes the great from the puny: that they can examine a thought, even from a child.

They talked of many things, these men, yet never of persons or of personalities. Their talk was of ideas, faith, hopes; of what the world might yet become with the vast knowledge which was then just coming into being. Among them each field had its champion — religion, geology, finance, news, communications, the grain for the good earth, the law, medicine, music, art.

When we had guests from the outside, these men listened with open minds: to Dr. Laubach with his great dream of each one teach one, that the world might read, and understand; to Dr. Mary Cushman, of *White Witch Doctor* fame, with indomitable faith in the healing way of her Lord and her uncanny way of conjuring the Gods of the jungle and the deep drums right up the aisle of the Watchung Avenue Congregational Church; to Mrs. Samango, whose father was a cannibal chief (he did not, she solemnly assumed me, wear a ring in his nose) and who was, I think, the most vital and unforgettable character I have ever met.

Missionaries from China, India, Burma, and Japan, from the Amazon, from the Congo, from Greenland, and from the teeming filthy jungles of our own city slums; people devoted to the service of man and to his well-being, came to our home to bring the good news to the parish, and slowly but irrevocably it was borne in on the heart and mind of a small child that the enormous debt which we owe to God lies not only in the death of Jesus of Nazareth but also in the lives of untold thousands who have served him and left us a legacy of all that we have that is worth-while.

We knew then that we could not afford to leave the vast continents of Asia and Africa neglected. But the practical people of the world said that we could not afford thousands of dollars for the salvation of savages. My morning paper in this year of our Lord 1954 informs me that we are now affording millions, not to mention lives.

It was not all deep and ponderous at Tongueslip. There was laughter, and stories and songs. Dad would sit with one leg

29

thrown over the arm of his deep, green chair playing the concertina, while Dr. Holland fiddled on his Stradivarius, which was one of the few such instruments I have ever heard put to the happy use for which it was intended. They are all too often kept in a safe, which is an ignominious fate for a beautiful voice. We would sing, not classics, not arias, but "Alouette," and "Carry Me Back to Old Virginny," and "Clementine," and sometimes the old familiar hymns.

It struck me even then as strange that many who to my knowledge had never darkened the doors of a church would sit by the fire at Tongueslip and sing the faith they lived though they did not profess it. They knew all the words, even the fifth and sixth and seventh verses, and I wondered, but did not dare ask, where they had learned them, and why they had remembered them.

It was because of these evenings around the fire that I presumed to move toward the occasion of a housewarming without consulting the Duchess. Everyone was sworn to secrecy, and Unkie and I fixed upon the date of January 20, Dad's and Mother's crystal anniversary.

We moved with infinite caution, speaking in conspiratorial whispers over the pages of Allen and Greenough's *Latin Grammar*. We plotted, we planned, we drew in the parish little by little, and when the Duchess, quite unconscious of it all, observed that the wedding anniversary must be kept in the family, since the parish had already done more than generously in matters of advice on the remodeling, and must not feel that they were obligated to come bearing gifts, Unkie and I sat with poker faces and assured her of our agreement.

The great day arrived. I was in a tizzy of anticipation. I had purchased a small glass mustard dish out of my own allowance, and could hardly wait for dinner to be over so that I could present it. Dinner never got over.

The Duchess became more and more conscious of a bustle of activity in the kitchen and went to investigate. There she found the maids and butlers of the parish laying out glasses and dishes, and, in the front parlor, the parish heavy-laden. The mayor, trading on his prerogative of Irish descent brought along two hundred feet of hose, and told Dad with a wink that the good Irish product to fill it would be along the next day. It was. There were fire irons, and bolts of sheeting, cut crystal punch cups, a beautiful mirror, plates for sandwiches, and so many gifts from loving friends that I trembled for my tiny mustard dish. It would, I knew, be lost in the midst of the lavish display of affection.

I gathered myself together to make my offering. There was dead silence in the room I thought. Children, I guess, always think of themselves as the cynosure. I know now that nobody noticed at all, except Dad and the Duchess. They thanked me kindly, and set the dish in the center of the mantelpiece, removing *the* Ming vase. My heart sang.

The old spinet tinkled, the accordion played, and Herman Hupfeld, later to gain fame as the composer of " Let's Put Out the Lights," played his violin. Four hundred people waltzed and bowed, chatted and visited, came and went in Tongue-slip that evening, and the house rocked with laughter and with song.

How nearly it rocked to disaster we did not discover until the workmen, repairing the ceiling in the cellar, called Dad down to ask his orders. He came upstairs white to the gills. The old ceiling had been pulled down and exposed the ends of the timbers. They were completely rotted off the foundation and hanging in mid-air. Nothing was holding up the floor but habit, and why it had not crashed through with the weight of the dancing parish only God knows. It is now supported by steel columns, and we dance on it with free breaths, but I was young then and did not know what we had been spared.

I only remember the heady sensation with which I read in the *Montclair Times* an account of the party, and the statement that I had given my parents a crystal mustard dish. It was the only gift mentioned by item and donor. *I had seen my name in print.* I wonder if ever again, under any circumstances, I shall be so moved by the power of the press.

[4]

I REMEMBER the day when the wild-goose weather vane went up on the barn. Dad sat astride the sagging ridgepole balancing the weather vane in one hand and lighting his pipe with the other.

His sandy hair curled in the breeze, and his lean hands stroked the painted feathers. "Your mother has done herself proud this time," he called down to me. "I can almost feel the gander's heart beat."

The hammer thudded and echoed against the shingles, and the wild goose swung slowly from west to north and back again. He *did* look real, and I loved him immediately. There is something about a wild goose that gets me where I live.

Dad reached into the pocket of his disreputable brown coveralls and took out a compass. He checked the position of the gilded *N* and grunted. "Compass says it's north." Then he squinted at the sun. "Sun says it's north." "If there are any objections speak now or else forever — "

It looked perfect and I said so. Dad edged toward the gable and a ripping sound betrayed the fact that a nail had caught in the already revealing hole in the seat of his pants.

He leaned over the edge of the roof and examined a large opening under the barn eaves. "It's well-worn. The barn owl must still be using it." He reached down and disengaged a tawny brown feather from a splinter and it drifted into my outstretched hands. Aluco the barn owl is one of my favorite birds, and I hoped against hope that she would raise her young again in the hayloft.

Mr. Slaight, our back door neighbor, had no such sentiments. He hated the owl and was determined to destroy her. The sound of methodical clipping informed us that Mr. Slaight was at work in his garden. Dad sidled back from the hole, an unnecessary precaution in view of the fact that Mr. Slaight knew where it was and aimed his shotgun at it with regularity. However at that moment he was concentrating on the few twigs of privet which had the temerity to grow outside of the carefully prescribed lines of his hedge.

Dad called down to him, "Hi, Neighbor."

Mr. Slaight neither looked up nor answered. I should have been surprised had he done so. He never had, and the chances of even this beautiful August morning breaking him down were slight.

Only a particularly savage snip of the shears betrayed the fact that he had heard. His blue-black hair and straight, thin mouth never deviated from their proper and compressed lines.

" I will say, ' good morning,' then, Herr Pastor."

The head of Ganz, the policeman, looked over the ridgepole like some fantastic puppet from a life-sized Punch-and-Judy show.

" How do you like your namesake, Ganz? "

Ganz examined the gander with care.

" *Schön,* Herr Pastor. But all is not well below."

Dad wrinkled his snub nose. " Why? What now? "

" Herr Slaight has phoned in that your bees take the sweetness from his flowers and drink all the water from his birdbath. Shall we see yet? "

The two men descended the ladder. I, being small and as curious as the Elephant's Child, snuck after them. They crossed the churchyard and went through the gate.

Mr. Slaight bowed reluctantly, and escorted them to an immaculate white marble shell, where a solitary bee struggled half-drowned in the water.

Dad shoved it ashore with his finger.

Mr. Slaight bit into his accusations like a meat chopper.

"You see what I mean, Officer — these bees are a nuisance, apt to sting people. I want this parson" — he pronounced the word as though it implied something from under a log — "to get rid of his hives."

I waited breathless for the explosion. I knew Dad would have dearly loved to clip the impeccable Mr. Slaight. I had always longed to shove him into a mud puddle. The way he swung his gloves and cane, his ubiquitous white spats, brought out the gutter rat in me. Dad only rubbed the back of his neck with his pipe stem and stared pointedly at the Red Astrachan tree, so laden with fruit that the limbs were propped against the weight.

Ganz looked at it too. He couldn't help seeing the product of the hive's labor any more than he could have failed to smell the tart fragrance of the windfalls. He started to pick up an apple, remained frozen, half-bent and staring. We all saw the glitter of the steel-trap ring, cunningly concealed among the fallen fruit.

We all knew where Lotor, my pet racoon, had disappeared to.

Ganz straightened slowly and the corners of his eyes were tight. He had scratched Lotor under the chin, and been licked lovingly in return. He had watched the little ring-tailed clown washing each morsel before he ate it and had laughted at his antics with the blackberry pail. Anger was in Ganz's voice, anger matching the surging fury within me.

"Herr Slaight, you are quite correct. There is a bee. Still remains a problem. Can we prove to the court that the bee belongs to the pastor? Without proof His Honor will sign no complaint."

Mr. Slaight set his jaw.

Dad tried desperately not to laugh.

Ganz saluted and led the way through the gate.

As I turned to scuttle around the barn, I heard the proper Hector Slaight say, "Goddammit," and saw him crush the semiconscious bee with a swipe of his gloves.

By the time I got around the corner Ganz was wiping the leather sweatband of his cap and mopping his face.

"*Donnerwetter!* Good Book or no, how is it that you do not murder such a neighbor?"

He stretched out his hand and picked a golden plum from Dad's pet tree, bit into it, and wiped the juice from his chin with the back of his hand.

Dad struck a match on the small remaining portion of his coverall seat, and puffed thoughtfully at his pipe. "I am always encouraged by the practical aspects of our faith, Ganz. Do you remember where Paul says, 'As much as in you lieth, be at peace with all men'? That gives one a bit of latitude."

And that gives you a pretty good picture of Mr. Slaight.

I think my chief complaint against him was that he threw countless blue Bromo Seltzer bottles into our back shrubbery. I had to pick them up. If I had been a little older, I might have caught the implication of the incessant consumption of antiacids, but in my happy childhood alcoholism was not a parlor topic. Some pitied the drunkard, but precious few people realized what everybody knows now. The result was that an endless series of maneuvers, social and ethical, complicted what might have been a relatively simple problem by the expedient of refusing to admit that it existed.

Anyhow Mr. Slaight caused me a lot of misery. He delighted in reporting the slightest deviation on my part to his wife, who promptly broadcast it to the whole neighborhood.

I remember one item with particular bitterness. There was a church dinner, and the pies were set on the window sill of the parish house to cool. Someone stole them and there was no dessert. Mr. Slaight vowed that I had taken them, and was believed. I was not only punished; I was treated for weeks with freezing civility by the Ladies' Aid. Cookies were given to me with the question, " Are they as good as the pies? " and then of course I could not even swallow them, let alone taste them.

I did *not* take those pies. It would never have entered my head to purloin them. Somehow in my mind, anything belonging to the church belonged to God. At that time I conceived of Him as a very much enlarged Deacon Martin, somewhere in the vicinity of a hundred feet high. If my moral fiber had been weak enough to succumb to the pies, my respect for this enormous and all-pervading Deity would have kept me from doing so.

Eventually the stigma of " pie stealer " retreated into the past as other and more heinous crimes were added to the list. I had only a few defenders. Among these was Dr. Arny, whose black eyes snapped when I was accused and who publicly lambasted one of the more caustic critics of my behavior while I stood stiff-legged and defiant beside him.

That was the day when someone put a row of empty whisky bottles on the church steps. By great good fortune I had been helping Mrs. Arny to turn the dasher for ice cream and my alibi was airtight.

I have not the slightest idea why I was turning Mrs. Arny's dasher. Probably because I loved being in her kitchen. It was different from other people's kitchens. It never smelled of cabbage or of fish, but always of rising bread, freshly ground coffee, and in winter of molasses taffy and Winesap apples.

Our home offered another sort of entertainment. On rainy days we could play in the barn, opening and examining the ancient trunks which Miss Lottie had not wanted and which the Duchess had put in the hayloft until such time as she could decently dispose of them. When this palled we would go down to the carriage house, where moisture had revived the warm smell of horses, lift down the saddles and bridles which still hung in the old tack room, fling them over the sawhorses, and ride off on journeys to far and wonderful places.

[5]

ONE of the many things which Robert, Malcolm, and I had turned up in the old trunks in the loft of the barn at Tongue-slip was a pile of photographs showing the house in various stages of growth and development. We had pored over them at long length, hoping to find errors in dimension that would reveal a secret passage, but all to no avail.

Christian Interest was supposed to have had such a hiding place, into which he retired when the Hessians passed through the area, but we have never been able to find one. There are panels that open, but none of them is big enough to hide anything larger than a rag doll. Still we studied the pictures, and Mother and Dad showed a proper enthusiasm.

One photograph, yellow and faded, was still remarkably clear. It showed an old lady seated on the steps, wearing a lace apron over her silk Sunday best and on her head a dainty lace cap. Beside her was a man in a frock coat and hard hat. Not far from where they sat was a well.

The ruts in the dirt of Oak Tree Lane were clear enough, and the neat flagstone path from the street to the front door was well-defined. A small sapling cherry had begun the growth which eventuated in the spreading branches shading the entire east side of the house, and which supplied the birds with a great many more cherries than we could ever harvest. In the photograph the tree looked precarious. Venetian blinds hung in the windows of the house, which surprised us. We had always thought of them as being comparatively modern.

Dad and the Duchess and I, of a spring Sunday, were trying to find out from exactly what point the picture had been taken, and were planning to pose in the same positions as the old couple ourselves. We thought it would be fun to duplicate the work of a photographer done on that sunny Sunday nearly a century before. We counted the flagstones to get the proper triangulation and suddenly Dad let out a war whoop.

"Look, Duchess! The flagstones are exactly the same. See that one — it's cracked smack across the northeast corner!"

He disappeared toward the barn and came back with a pickax and a long-handled shovel. "Let's find the well."

I counted. "Eighteen flagstones due north, and about as wide as the last one east."

The shovel bit into the sod; a neat round hole about a foot in diameter was made. I grabbed the pick, but Mother stopped me. "Easy does it. If you break off the pipe, we'll never be able to locate it."

Dad used the shovel carefully. Up came the turf, roots clinging tenaciously to mother earth, and we scraped the hole deeper. Metal hit metal with a clang, and we worked gently with our hands. The Duchess felt it first. Her fingers were more sensitive than Dad's and mine, and she uncovered it, triumphantly, a two-inch pipe, capped neatly against the ravages of time.

We had the well, but what were we to do with it? Was it possible that after all these years there was anyone left in Montclair who could fix it so that it would work? We held a council of war. Why not look in the yellow pages of the phone book? And so we did.

We not only uncovered the well; we uncovered a multitude of fascinating occupations. Reading the yellow pages is like reading the dictionary. You always get sidetracked by something interesting and unexpected that you had not intended to find at all. Did you think that fletchers, those men who put feathers on arrows, had gone out with Robin Hood? Well, they aren't all gone by a long shot. They are listed in the yellow pages.

Blacksmiths, chair caners, marriage brokers, and midwives rub shoulders with television repairers and atomic manufacturing companies. Only the clergy, the pharmacists, the physicians, and the undertakers remain fairly static in numbers. There is probably a profound philosophical truth to be found in the yellow pages. Someday I shall pursue it.

There are still people who dig and repair wells. We called one. He arrived promptly, which is in itself remarkable, in an ancient Star, which was even more remarkable in that it spouted a geyser of water from the radiator cap, a kind of rolling advertisement.

"Yuzzer," he could fix the pump. It would cost a hundred dollars, but it could be done. He would come next day, and in the meantime would we please read these pamphlets. We sat down prepared to absorb statistics on lift and priming, and found ourselves faced with a pile of religious tracts dealing largely with the evils of alcohol. The man who dug wells was obviously putting his beliefs into practice. It must be wonderful to have found a truly practical solution to your most profound convictions.

On the other hand I don't imagine he could earn a decent living at it. A recent survey of water supply in case of atomic attack reveals only six wells in our town. The income per annum on their maintenance must be low. Air conditioning helps a little, one supposes. I know Hahne and Company on Church Street has a tremendous artesian well for its conditioner.

Anyhow, he came back the next day. He had two men and a derrick. The rig was attached to his truck and skewgeed off to the side so that the entire apparatus gave the impression of a colossal crab sidling down the road. They managed to squeeze the outfit between the pine tree and the house and to maneuver it into position without taking any corners off the roof. Then they fastened chains to the pipe and started an intricate series of motions calculated to pull it up. The pipe held fast. Christian Interest or his heirs had used excellent materials. Nothing would induce the line to budge.

Finally it was decided to run a pipe of slightly smaller diameter down the inside of the original line. Section was screwed to section, and down it went: thirty feet, forty feet, fifty, and finally eighty feet, where it stopped short with a crunching bump.

The well was driven through the sandstone and igneous bedrock upon which our town stands. There was not the slightest danger of surface contamination. The pump was affixed, and the handle stroked. Up gurgled the water, slimy, rusty, and foul! We could have wept. The exponent of temperance, the salesman of Adam's ale, came sympathetically to our comfort.

"Dun't ee wuzzy. There's only old pipe broked off. 'Ere now, give 'er a pull."

We pumped in turns, each giving the handle a hundred strokes. We pumped all morning, we pumped all afternoon, we called in the kids and the neighbors. By evening we thought we could see some improvement in the water, but there was none in our backs. Sleep was impossible. A thousand muscles unknown to modern science screamed from unaccustomed use. Blistered palms and blistering disappointment combined to complete our misery. In the morning we started to pump again. Suddenly out of the spigot poured pails full of rusty mud, and then as suddenly it cleared and ran like a mountain stream, cold, clean, pure. I ran for a pitcher, and the water pouring into it frosted the silver initials. We drank deep drafts, and our backs forgot to hurt.

We, with our pump, were just in time. Within a week the town water came under suspicion because of a terrific outbreak of intestinal disease. It all stemmed back to a government directive, which is something a good many people may find surprising. Evidently the brilliance of these documents is not confined to the period most caustically blamed for them in Republican circles!

This particular stroke of genius decreed that Jersey City was to have more water. The fact that the filtering plant was already operating at top capacity was not taken into consideration. The town got water right out of the Passaic River, unfiltered, and loaded with chlorine so that it smelled like the sheets boiling on washday. B. coli will succumb to chlorine, B. welchii will not, and the town was smitten even as the hosts of Alexander were smitten in that portion of the Anabasis where they plundered the old honey from the hives of Greece. Dr. North spotted the difficulty in Montclair, and he had everyone boiling the water and fairly well cleared up within a few days. However, when it had been boiled the resemblance to Monday's washtub was enhanced and it was difficult if not impossible to swallow the nauseous brew.

Water, plain ordinary drinking water, was at a premium. The neighborhood beat a path to our well. Many people offered to pay for the privilege of using the pump, but Dad and the Duchess felt that such capitalization upon a common disaster was, to put it mildly, hardly ethical. They refused to consider the offer.

The Slaights were susceptible to the same organisms as the rest of humanity and, like all other living creatures, needed water. Even Hector Slaight could not survive for long without the liquid which he never touched except when mixed with Bromo Seltzer! He was faced, for the first time in his life, with a basic problem. Money had always solved his problems, and he expected that it would solve this one too. He wrote to Dad, on embossed stationery, which was his first error, and stated flatly that he did not wish to be beholden to us. For that I rather liked him; he was at least consistent!

Dad replied, on church stationery, that water was a gift of God, not to be sold, and sent me over with the message that

41

if Mr. Slaight would not come to get the water, we would leave it on his back porch daily.

Mrs. Slaight found the tactful solution to the impasse. She was wise enough to know that two stubborn men would not reach any agreement over so touchy a matter, and she made a flat proposition to me.

"Mary, we have to have water. Now, you take this dollar, go buy some jugs, and deliver me three gallons a day. I will scrub the jugs, and you shall have a nickel a jug for delivering it. That will satisfy everybody. Your father won't be selling water; Mr. Slaight won't be asking favors. This entire thing is so silly that only you and I can solve it."

I looked at her in amazement. I had never really looked at her before. I did not really understand what I saw — the lines around her eyes, the whiteness around her lips, the lost look of utter defeat — but somehow I knew what she meant, and was for the first time sorry for my enemy.

The Duchess and I had a council of war, and approached Dad obliquely. Here, said the Duchess, was an opportunity for me to learn the value of money. Here was a chance to get an understanding of business practice. Dad agreed that if that was the way Mrs. Slaight wanted it, he had better give in. No use making any more difficulty for her. Business boomed.

After further discussion it was deemed allowable, in the case of people who wanted the same arrangement as the Slaights', for me to deliver water. Nevertheless it must remain understood — and a sign so stating must be placed on every jug — that water was free to those who wished to come and get it.

My printing press was put to work, and labels, agreements, and statements run off. Business hit the top of the chart. I had to have help!

Thus was born the first Travis-Arny combination. Robert's younger brother, Malcolm, the one who wanted to know about where Dad had shot the babies, had an express wagon, and

Robert, who had been neat from the cradle, carefully lettered on the side, TRA-ARN WATER COMPANY.

A nickel a jug for delivery, and people scrubbed their own bottles! We coined money. Ten dollars a week was average; in hot weather it hit fifteen and twenty. We really pulled that little red wagon around. Robert built a top deck for it to save us trips. It never occurred to us to pay him. It seldom does! Malcolm always had money for a baseball, bat, or crystal for his radio. I always had cash on hand for triangular stamps and printing equipment. I spent my money with profligate extravagance, and, even when I had no more cash, Robert, still kind and patient, showed me where Adam Morgan's dump was so that I could rescue discarded radio parts and build sets along with the other fellows. Dad insisted that I bank a fair percentage of my earnings.

I still have a billhead, on which the make-up is patently amateur, for the Tra-Arn Water Company; I still have the bankbook in which my deposits are listed; but Robert may comfort himself. Now as then he is the backbone of the enterprise, patiently, quietly, loyally keeping things going, filling the gaps, picking up the pieces, the reason and the strength behind everything and anything I do. He is the buyer of baseballs, bats, and sodas for the Tra-Arn Company now, and he is still showing us all where we can get things, and how to build for ourselves.

Eventually Montclair linked in with a new and pure water supply, and business dwindled, but to this day there is a dipper and a bucket beside the pump. Each spring the sound of its squeaking handle can be heard as thirsty workmen, thirsty children, and thirsty passers-by stroke the cold water from the deep stone well. The bucket is for horses, of which there are still a few, and it is always kept full for dogs. They do not seem to mind the floating oats; rather, they seem to relish the flavor on their lolling tongues.

Two handles have been worn through since the day Mrs.

43

Slaight and I made a deal. The old gourd dipper is lost, and I have never been able to get another. Like the horse, the gourd is a vanishing thing in a world that has little time to pump water by hand and is willing to forego the fresh, clear stream of life for the less effortless way of having it pumped and chlorinated by somebody else.

[6]

TONGUESLIP not only has a pump and a barn. It has outbuildings of all shapes, sizes, and descriptions, mentionable and unmentionable. These Dad put into a semblance of repair himself, and over the years each has developed a name according to its use.

The goosehouse is probably the most puzzling to strangers, for although it contains the few items in the world that are not in the barn, and duplicates of some that are, it has not a honk, a feather, or a hiss of a goose. Once, however, the story was different.

Dad went hunting one cold November day, and on his way back through the country a sign caught his eye.

FRESH BUTTERMILK
DONKEY EGGS
for sale

He always liked buttermilk, but it was the donkey eggs that were the bait. Who could resist the impulse to discover one of those? He got only as far as the barnyard, where a burly farmer was struggling with a goose and finding it impossible to get goose, ax, and chopping block into proper position. Dad watched the process for a bit, decided that the goose was smarter than the farmer, and offered to buy the creature alive.

44

The farmer, who by this time was sweating, furious and embarrassed, seized the offer avidly, and Dad became the proud possessor of one large gray Toulouse goose, which he brought home to me for a pet.

For some obscure reason it was promptly named Hike, and because the little red building with the green roof and the louvered cupola was unoccupied, Hike was installed therein and it became "the goosehouse."

Whoever coined the phrase "silly as a goose" may have known something about semantics but had a wealth of ignorance about geese.

Hike was extraordinarily intelligent. He followed me around like a dog, and made most pleasant and engaging conversational noises. Hike was housebroken, and never made a social error. Hike was soft, and his down against my cheeks was often comfort against the heartbreaks of childhood.

One fine spring morning Hike came through with *his* final triumph. He laid an egg, a large beautiful white egg. Not quite complete, definitely lacking calcium at one end of the shell, but undoubtedly holding promise of a better and more fertile product. I was in seventh heaven. All we needed was a gander, and we could have goslings.

The family were singularly unenthusiastic. Mr. Slaight had already complained about Hike's soft honking, which, I admit, rose to a crescendo if anyone trespassed after dark, but I was twelve and determined.

I waited until a propitious moment when the Duchess was at a meeting of the Ladies' Aid and Dad had a funeral. This I knew would give me an afternoon free from interruption and an evening when Dad would not have the energy to call me to order. Funerals always left him exhausted. He felt the burdens of others more deeply perhaps than his own.

I gathered my wealth from my bank, a model of the old Flatiron Building, hopped a bus, where fortunately I did not quite come up to the mark on the door and so had to pay only half fare, and rode the ten joggling, nausea-producing miles to Newark. There, in the market, I knew I would find a gander.

The Old Market Building was redolent of cheese and herring, filled with a motley crew of vendors of vegetables, eggs, meat and poultry, rabbits, chickens, and ducks. I almost succumbed to a white Angora rabbit, but the honking of geese in the distance steadied me, and I went on.

The geese had already been plucked, and were walking around with their backsides bare, like small children in sleepers several sizes too large. This, I assumed, should make it a cinch for me to get a gander. The evidence was clearly exposed. I entered into consultation with a Hungarian gooseherd, whose enormous handle-bar mustache, gruff voice, and accent, which you could have cut with a knife, would have dimmed a lesser determination. Together we upended goose after goose, and came at last to a unanimous decision. I made my purchase. I think now that he must have been grinning behind his shrubbery. He sold me that goose for sixty-three cents!

Alexander the Gander was placed rear first in a paper bag with his head sticking out, and a bright red ribbon tied around the neck of the bag and the neck of the goose to keep them from parting. With this concoction under my arm, I proudly strode the streets of Newark to the bus stop.

One of the joys of childhood is its sublime unawareness of eccentricity. It is natural to want things, and it makes no difference what anybody else thinks about the logic or the protocol of the problem. If the good people at Newark stared at the sight of a small, redheaded, freckle-faced girl with pigtails and a tip-tilted nose carrying a live and honking goose in a paper bag, I do not remember it. I had my goose. That was enough. I wish that an adult could retain that happy serenity of oblivion.

We got home and into the goosehouse before Dad and

Mother returned, but the more I looked at that naked rear, the more embarrassed I became for Alexander the Gander. Finally I dressed Alexander in a pair of blue sailor pants, borrowed from my favorite doll. It was this phenomenal sight, waddling down the driveway after Hike, which met the astonished eyes of the disbanding Ladies' Aid.

All went well for a while with Alexander and Hike. They knew that they were not allowed in the garden, and if they were there, they refused to answer when called. The minute they had passed its border they set up a honking and yacking, and pelted, with wings flapping and necks outstretched, into my arms, to be petted and fed with tidbits of Unkie's delectable celery.

On one occasion their popularity was seriously dimmed. That was the day when, with the thermometer standing at ninety in the shade, Unkie planted two rows of very special beans. Hike and Alexander waited for him to leave the garden, and then promptly and efficiently followed down the drills and ate each and every seed. Unkie saw them from the bathroom window, but his sense of propriety was such that he could not chase them clad only in a bath towel. By the time he got his pants on, the damage was completed. Unkie ate his *pâté de foie gras* with a fierce and vengeful expression that night. I was really worried!

At about this time Dad became very much interested in metaphysics. He was always off on some subject that seemed far removed from the church, but always turned out to have a profound relationship to it. The large and erudite tooled-leather volume on this particular variety of black magic contained long lists of experimental evidence calculated to impress the armchair sorcerer's apprentice. One of the most interesting of these items concerned a goose. It gave explicit directions for an exercise designed to prove conclusively that charms and shibboleths have reality and effectiveness.

One was to place the goose, with its head under its wing,

at a point marked with a cross. After the goose was in position, you took a piece of chalk and drew a circle six feet in diameter around it. Then you turned the goose around three times from left to right, three times from right to left, and repeated the prescribed charm with each rotation. The theory was that the goose would then be unable to cross the chalk line and would remain in the circle until released by a second incantation.

If the Ladies' Aid had been astounded by the sight of a goose in blue sailor pants walking down the driveway of the manse, you can imagine their confusion, yea, their viewing with alarm, the sight of their pastor holding an enormous red volume, drawing a six-foot chalk mark around a goose whose head was being held under its wing by their pastor's wife. But they were not more astonished than the author of the book would have been.

The goose was unimpressed. It walked out of the circle honking every time we said the magic words.

Probably the people who read erudite books on metaphysics are not supposed to keep geese, and it was expected that the experiment would be accepted as valid on faith. The author did not know the parson of Tongueslip. It was not for nothing that he was named Thomas. He followed his apostolic predecessor as though indeed he had been his twin.

However, the charm may have been for another purpose. The next day Alexander the Gander laid a nice big, round, white egg.

Geese were by no means the only creatures at Tongueslip. Every ragtag and bobtail of a stray animal sought and found welcome there. Only one rule obtained. If any creature created noise or smell, it had to be trained or cleansed or disposed of. "It is not," the Duchess averred, "the animals that are dirty, it is the folks that keep them."

Uncle Jim, of whom more later, was constantly bringing me turtles and frogs from swamps drained to reduce the population of the famous New Jersey mosquitoes. Uncle Jim earned his living bossing a gang who ditched and sprayed. Why New Jersey should be singled out for the dubious honor of having stingers is still a question in my mind. They are much worse in Portsmouth, New Hampshire, and in Canada I have seen places where you can't open your mouth without swallowing fifty of them. But, be that as it may, Uncle Jim drained swamps and brought me the livestock therefrom.

He also brought me a pair of parakeets; handsome brutes, not small and dainty like the current budgies, but some ten inches high, green, orange and crimson, with dispositions quite as loud as their feathers.

Someone, sometime, must have treated them abominably, for they were vicious, vindictive, and completely untamable. We kept them in the small greenhouse at first, but they tore the contents and the doorframes to shreds and we were forced to relegate them to a cage.

Dad abhorred cages. It was his theory that any creature, properly treated, could be taught to behave in a proper manner and permitted to wander the house untrammeled. Cages, physical, mental, and spiritual, were to him anathema. He could not and would not endure the sight of anything that curtailed freedom. He demanded it for all, and observed its boundaries as scrupulously for others as for himself. If Voltaire had not already written it, Dad would have coined the saying, " Though I passionately disagree with everything you say, I will defend to the death your right to say it."

This extended to the parakeets. One fine spring day he opened the cage door and set them free.

When I got home I was beside myself, and Dad was abjectly apologetic. He acknowledged that he had trespassed, that the birds were mine in so far as any living creature could be said to belong to anyone. He had let them go.

He filled the cage with sunflower seed, took me by the hand, and we started north in the direction of their flight.

49

Whistling and calling, the parson of Tongueslip, cage in one hand and sobbing child by the other, trudged the streets of Montclair, looking for the parakeets.

It was hot and the streets were dusty. Sweat-stained and tear-begrimed the two of us searched until sunset, and after that until dark. Only an occasional derisive laugh, which we thought to be the birds', but might well have been human, reached our ears.

Finally, exhausted, we came home. The battle was lost, and the Duchess had peace to restore. Somehow she managed it.

The next morning Unkie called to me and to Dad, who came running, still buttoning his trousers, " Quick, Mary, look out your window! "

I did. The peach tree was in full bloom. Dew hung on every coral petal. And placidly perched in its boughs, almost ethereal in their beauty, were the prodigal parakeets.

They flew serenely into their cage, settled down to a hearty meal, and never improved one wit in either vocabulary or disposition.

It was shortly after this that Dad's passionate championship of equal rights for animals almost caused a murder.

He was walking with Lem. Lem who had taken such good care of us while Dad was at war. Lem who had guarded Tongueslip when it was wide open to thieves. Lem who had pointed many a handsome pheasant. Lem the gentleman dog, with an educated heart. He had just crossed the street and was standing with his paws on the curb waiting for Dad, when a taxi driver of low degree and deliberate intentions came driving like Jehu down the avenue. He deliberately swerved to hit the dog. Lem flew through the air and struck his head on a low stone wall. Blood poured from his muzzle, his eyes glazed.

Dad jumped onto the running board of the cab, seized the driver by the collar, and hauled him out. The car hit the wall and stalled. Dad walloped the everlasting daylights out of a man half again his size.

Then he went to look at Lem. A pink tongue licked his hand, and Dad picked up the tattered dog in his arms and wept. Fortunately the damage, though gory, was not fatal. If I read correctly the worn inscription on the dog graves under the apple tree, it was not until 1926 that Lem went to the happy hunting grounds.

As is inevitable, he came into the house one night, crossed his paws, put down his head, and looked up at Dad. "What's the trouble, old boy? Tired?" Lem thumped his tail and closed his eyes. His paws twitched across the fields that are forever green, where men are always young, where the trout rise in the early mists of a perpetual April, and where even a well-bred setter may desert birds and chase rabbits to his heart's content.

We knew we should never find another dog like Lem. As Dad said, "No man deserves to have but one dog like that." But we searched the kennels of America from Florida to Maine. We were prejudiced, I know, but there just wasn't a dog we could really love. Dad and Deacon Martin talked incessantly about setters, and the deacon's white crop whiskers moved sympathetically up and down. He was a kindly man, if awe-inspiring, and he made a constructive suggestion.

"Doctor, you have done all you could yourself. I think now it is time to pray. Time to ask the Lord to send you a dog. I am sure He would understand."

So to our evening prayers and petitions was added, "And, our Father, please send us another dog, not as good as Lem — that's asking too much — but a dog we can really love."

Perhaps such a petition from a pastor was unique, and therefore interesting. In any case it received instant attention.

The next morning a telegram arrived from the Wyandank Club: "Enjoyed your lecture on riding bull moose. Are sending along token of appreciation. Directors last night voted you one setter. Call American Express."

51

That afternoon Deacon Martin came in proudly leading a pair of lemon and white Llewellins. " My next door neighbor's wife hates 'em. They leave white hairs on the carpets. They're yours."

Two days later a friend called. " My son has asthma. The doctor says we have to get rid of our dog. I know you want one. Would you care to give Roderick Dhu a home?"

We now had four dogs, all handsome, all well trained, but Uncle Jim thought I should have a treasure of my own. He brought Flo along. She was the most beautiful Irish setter I have ever seen. Her red coat was like milkweed down, her feathers stood out in the slightest breath of air. She carried her head like a queen, and was, except that she was a little fat, a thing of beauty and a joy forever.

Uncle Jim put her in the box stall in the stable.

Feeding those dogs was getting to be expensive. We couldn't afford to buy meat for five large and hungry creatures. Dad went to Louis, the chef at the Inn. We always had large boxes of Corona Coronas, each individual cigar packed in a glass tube, each luxurious box the gift of a grateful parishioner. Dad was a pipe smoker, and to Unkie's horror used to cut these gems into one-inch pieces and let them burn slowly and extravagantly in his meerschaum. Louis was a connoisseur of cigars, and one box of Corona Coronas settled the dog food problem. Louis saved the scraps from the table, and I collected them in buckets drawn in the Tra-Arn express wagon. Wages weren't what " they used to was." For this task I got the sumptuous sum of ten cents a week.

I hurried home to feed the dogs and collect. Brimming pan in hand, I went first to call upon Flo in the box stall, and there dropped the meal with a splash and splatter in the deep bed of straw.

Flo had had a record litter of eleven puppies!

I shouted for Dad and the Duchess, who came running. We each took a pup in our arms and cuddled it. I can feel the warmth and delight of its ecstatic wriggling, and the small pink tongue running over my hands, to this day.

Dad stood for a moment looking down at Flo and the nursing puppies nuzzling close against her. The corners of his gray eyes crinkled as he knelt in the straw, took off his hat, and said very quietly:

"Thank you, Lord; that is enough dogs now, Sir."

[7]

"A REVOLT in Bavaria, organized by General Ludendorf and Adolf Hitler, has been put down. Hitler, an insignificant pawn in the plot, is presently imprisoned in Landsberg."

The signals were faint on my radio, but the great thing had been accomplished; I had built a machine that would pick up London!

I don't know whether or not children in other towns were as wireless-conscious as we were. Perhaps our interest in a wide new world may have stemmed from Adam Morgan's dump heap.

The contraptions that we concocted would have put Rube Goldberg to shame and most of the switches and dials on the panels we made had no other function than to bewilder our parents. Dials were plentiful, as were cat whiskers, coils, and audion tubes which glowed like the lights in our children's spaceships. I guess kids don't change much. It is amazing how gadgets impress people. We spent our afternoons at the dump collecting them.

This miraculous pile of twisted wire, bakelite, insulators, and floor sweepings engaged every minute of our time, from school out to dark. Seldom has an occupation been more revealing. The big boys would pitch each other unceremoniously off the heap, fighting and clawing for precedence, but the south side of the dump was reserved for small fry like myself. Our rights and privileges in the matter of treasure trove were scrupulously respected. Nothing, however good, was snatched from us. It was a gentlemen's agreement and the kids stuck to it.

What was even more surprising was that the older boys often helped the rest of us in such dangerous enterprises as putting aerials in trees.

I remember that one of the fellows, then twelve, but now a designer of guided missiles, was doing a little practice climbing. He had a neighbor not quite three, up an enormous maple tree, happily perched on a precarious limb some thirty feet in the air.

His father came home from work and saw the two of them. He paused for a split second, realized that if he scared the baby he would certainly fall, and shouted up to his son, " GET THAT BABY DOWN OUT OF THAT TREE! "

He then, according to his own statement, retired to the house and stood with his stomach churning and sweat pouring down his back, while his son obeyed orders.

Fortunately operation maple tree was brought to a successful conclusion. Most of Connie's ventures are — a fact which makes me sleep better nights.

Ninth-grade boys look so old when you are small, and seem so young when you are their mother! But still they solder lightning switches and adjust spark coils with consummate skill. We used to get the coils from the junkie, who removed them from Model T Fords.

The Federal Communications Commission had not yet been invented. We sent messages to our hearts' content. Conversation consisted, then as now, of descriptions of our setups and of circuits.

The first written communication from me to Robert concerned a crystal. He kept the note, and I found it not long ago, in his jewelry box. It reads precisely thus:

"Roburt, I took the big galeena chrystal. Love Mary."

Evidently, even then, as on the day I was borrowing his cuff links and discovered the early evidence, I had sublime faith that he would share with me the best he had. Still, looking at it from my present vantage point, I wonder at my colossal crust. A really sensitive crystal was a treasure not lightly to be filched. It was a crucial item, the all-important heart of the radio receiver.

Headphones presented quite a problem. I got mine by the simple, but long-drawn-out, expedient of saving United Cigar Store coupons. In this, as in many enterprises, Hans Folkers aided and abetted me. Mr. and Mrs. Folkers lived at the Marlboro Inn, and so had access to a great many people. Once my wants were known, coupons were "saved for Mary." I garnered them in wholesale lots and had two sets of headpieces.

Eventually we got a loud-speaker for the set, and it was moved into the Pine Room. A hideous black horn was suspended from the molding and music poured forth with sufficient audibility to interrupt conversation. The Duchess never liked it. "It reminds me of those trumpets at the Society for Psychical Research." As a matter of fact, it wasn't so very different after all. Who knows but one day we shall all have communication with each other across time as well as across space?

I can remember how people laughed at me when I set up wires to listen to England. I can even remember my great-aunt who was pitied when she insisted upon becoming engaged to a "lunatic who is interested in flying machines," and I know a very old lady whose father told her brother that he would disown him if he were "such a fool as to take half interest in Mr. Alexander Graham Bell's ridiculous toy for fifteen hundred dollars." One almost concludes from the evidence of history that only the fools were right! Perhaps laughter is the greatest compliment!

Audubon was the butt of a good deal of humor when he

banded the famous phoebes at Mill Grove, and birders still strike a lot of people as funny. Birdbanders are dismissed as being pathological. I still wish I had banded Aluco the barn owl. She has raised thirty broods since the days when I was hugging geese and making radios, and I would give a good deal to know whether the last incumbent of the loft was her daughter or her granddaughter. My only chance to find out was destroyed when the last brood was slaughtered and left to rot at the base of the wall, but I suppose that things like that are a part of life and must not be taken too bitterly to heart, if one can help it!

It was Robert who went into the loft with me to band Aluco's grandchildren. He didn't want me to get hurt. I remembered then what I thought I had forgotten — the first time he came to my defense.

There was a pumpkin field in the lot across the corner, and a good many of the kids had partaken of the potential jack-o'-lanterns. They were mostly the same fellows who went to the dump, built radios, and swapped stamps with me. I remembered their fairness at the treasure pile, but I had forgotten how thoroughly they did me at the stamp trading. One in particular really took me over in the matter of the Gabon cannibal chief, and it was he who was the prime mover in *l'affaire* pumpkin.

We had a big burlap sack and it was pretty well filled, but there was one walloping big pumpkin across the rows which it would take three kids to lift. I was too small for that job, so I was left literally holding the bag.

The boys, thoroughly experienced in such matters, heard Old Man Lousybugger coming through the corn. I was inexperienced and waited for a signal to extricate me from my precarious position. Alas, it did not come! The fellows took to their heels and left me to face Lousybugger alone.

I was collared and given a thorough going over, but the old man was, after all, merciful and did not give me the thrash-

56

ing I richly deserved. However, he did threaten to call the police. I went home in tears, and Mother, who was in bed with the flu, could not make head or tail of my sobbing story. I insisted that the man's name *was* Lousybugger, and my elegant mother, quite as unfamiliar with the back-fence jargon of adolescence as I was, tried to find it in the telephone book.

I shudder to think of the expression of horror that must have frozen the face of "Information" when the minister's wife carefully spelled out that name! For of course we couldn't find it in the directory.

The next day, shaking but still able to swagger — for had I not been threatened by the cops? — I made my way homeward from school. Unwise in my frankness from the very beginning, I taunted the older boys for running away and bragged of my own indomitable courage, which had been due to the fact that my feet were paralyzed with terror. I was receiving my just deserts when Robert happened along. I don't know what he did to my assailants, but they melted away like hailstones in a summer storm, and Robert, bless him, picked me up, wiped my face, and took me home, safe from the consequences of my own misdeeds.

From that day forward I looked upon him with awe and affection.

One cannot stay a child forever. Dad and Robert could not always absorb my blows for me.

Times changed. The town grew. Where once there had been open fields filled with blue gentians, there were houses, row after row. Unkie was dead, and the X-ray which might have saved him was so commonplace that it was used for fitting shoes. Mother was running a business. Dad was away a great deal on lecture tours, and they both felt that, although I had a great many friends, the fact that they were all boys implied that even the influence of Miss Edythe and Miss Helen had not made sufficient impact upon my hoyden heart. I wore taffeta, but only under protest, and was even then apt to have

57

corduroy knickers beneath my rustling skirts. The sound of swishing taffeta and whistle britches, so Nell DeGolyer tells me, was an odd one! I seem to have worn same to a birthday party at her home. I had to be sent to a proper school and taught to behave like a 'ady instead of like the seven sons which the Duchess had dreamed of bearing. I was shipped off to Miss Beard's School, where the reformation was begun.

I think I have never known anyone whom I both loved and feared as I did Miss Beard. She was a miraculous character, tall, white-haired, straight as a ramrod, and as unyielding in her precepts and standards as that proverbial tool.

She had two watchwords: "Remember that you are to the manner born," and, "Life is a boomerang." I don't know that I still agree with the first, but experience has taught me that the second was correct in every detail.

Miss Beard could not abide sloppiness of any variety, mental, spiritual, or physical. We pressed, we polished, we learned, we behaved, and we did it twenty-four hours a day for four years. It became, not a matter of education, but a matter of habit.

Miss Beard abhorred high heels. She abominated lipstick and rouge. I realize now that she had a system, and that there was method to the madness which sometimes produced a call to her office and sometimes did not. If she could not see your rouge and lipstick, your technique was acceptable. These cosmetics were from her viewpoint, not immoral, but things to be used with restraint.

Her educational standards extended to the bathtub, and I think that in the four years when I knew her best the thing that upset her the most radically was that she once found *two* rings in the bathtub. That one of us could have left a tub without washing it was bad enough, but that anyone could have taken a bath in that tub without removing the diabolical evidence of previous use was unthinkable barbarianism.

Miss Beard educated us and we stayed educated. One supposes that to be "finished" implies very little of importance, but I must confess that what I learned from her has been a good deal more practical than most of the other book "larnin'" I have absorbed at one university or another.

The ability to plot the curve of an equa.ion is not as useful as the knowledge of how to keep tea hot over a long period of time. A knowledge of the principle upon which a ball bounces cannot be compared to the value of familiarity with the fact that a courteous approach to a salesman, a cook, or a laundress is apt to produce results.

Of course we translated Caesar and Vergil. Certainly we learned that the square on the hypothenuse of a right-angle triangle is equal to the sum of the squares on the other two sides, and we memorized lengthy portions of *Hamlet, Macbeth,* and *The Merchant of Venice.* I dare say that this had a very practical value too. Many is the time when I have had a decision to make and Portia has spoken firmly in my ear, "The quality of mercy is not strain'd."

I can never hear the tinkle of a dinner bell without falling silent. That was Miss Beard's method of conveying the fact that our voices were too strident. Alas, living for years with people who are deaf has now produced in me a habitual roar, and much public speaking to clubs has not improved the silver tones with which I express my opinions! Nevertheless I do know that a voice "ever soft, gentle, and low" is "an excellent thing in woman."

I never open my Bible but I smooth the pages: "The Bible is the sum of all human experience, and should be so treated."

Nobody ever got out of Miss Beard's School without a thorough knowledge of the Bible. She looked upon that book as the prime requisite for literacy. Its contents, to her, had a proper place of precedence in the world, and here I had a head start. I knew it from Genesis to Revelation. I was as a freshman, a mere neophyte, often invited to her house for dinner purely on that account. I loved her from the bottom of my heart because I respected her from the same area.

I am getting a little ahead of myself here, but this seems as good a place as any to tell it. Robert and I went to the golden anniversary of the school. We sat near Miss Beard, and I saw that Robert was watching her, trying to puzzle something out. Finally his face brightened and the funny little furrow between his eyes disappeared. " I have it! "

Miss Beard leaned over, as ever aware of every guest and every gesture.

" You have what, Robert? "

" What is different here. There is a room full of women and not one of them is trying to outshout the rest! "

" That," said dear Lucie, " justifies my fifty years as a headmistress."

I think, if I may say so, that there was a great deal more than that to justify it. I know for instance that in my case she went to the college which I had entered and personally saw the dean and the faculty. I know that she made a straight path before me, wherever I went, as long as she lived, and I am sure that she did it for others.

As to college, well, I survived it.

It was Professor Fiske and Miss Butters who saved me from despair. They were my friends, and their home was my abiding place. I always got along with deans and professors. My problems arose with instructors, still slightly damp behind the ears. These young and inexperienced individuals were entirely bound by the book. College is supposed to teach you to think, but they threw constant obstacles in the way. Their method was: memorize the book! I dare say I gave them a rough time asking, quite innocently at first, what the book was trying to convey. When I discovered that they didn't know, I took a diabolical delight in embarrassing them. Therefore I probably deserved what I got, which was cordial dislike and a majority of contra votes in faculty meeting.

The Department of Science also had instructors, but I soon

discovered the way to get around that. If you took problems courses, you got the full professors. I majored in problems in Botany, and minored in problems in Zoology. What a miracle of wonder Professor Hausman and Professor Fiske laid before my newly opened eyes!

Professor Hausman is an ornithologist of note. You may have read some of his books. I supplied some of the material for him in the form of jumping over a rail fence and breaking my nose on the binoculars which, hung from a strap around my neck, flew up and caught me a terrific clip. Dr. Hausman cautions beginners against just this bit of flamboyance.

My friendship with him nearly came to a bitter end in the matter of a tarantula. Someone had found this lovely specimen on a bunch of bananas and brought it to him. It was a tremendous one, as big as a saucer, and it got out in the lab. Only the assistant and I knew it was out, as there seemed no necessity of causing a panic.

The assistant, Dr. Hausman, and I were helping in the freshman lab. Suddenly a big, black, hairy tarantula landed on the paper in front of me. I admit it, I nearly fainted. The world swam, and I saw stars. Then the assistant laughed. She had taken the dry specimen from the case and dumped it to scare me. I was livid. What I said to her would have made *From Here to Eternity* sound like a pink tea.

Dr. Hausman gave me one scathing look and walked out. It was a good many weeks before I was asked to a lab tea again!

I think the first thing that curdled the Department of Mathematics was that I was unceremoniously flunked in that subject in my freshman year. This made me a freshman until I had passed a re-exam, and I had to sit with the freshmen in chapel. This was an ignominy that I did not propose to endure, and I went to the department asking for a waiver. It was curtly refused. So I set to work on a devious plot to circumvent that.

There must be some way out of it, I was sure. I cut chapel

and watched to see how it worked. Light dawned. All I had to do was join the choir. I cannot read music, but Lois Bloom, now Duckworth, my roommate, could, and she could play anything in the world if she heard it once.

I went down to the music room and got the choirmaster's book. Lois and I spent the next week on that subject exclusively. I memorized the alto of every single anthem Mr. Newton ever used in chapel, and I went to the tryouts, and was accepted with open arms. For, said Music Master Newton, "your ability to read music amounts almost to genius. There is a career for you in *a cappella!*" I never disabused him, and I never sat with the freshmen. The Department of Mathematics had been foiled and knew it!

Junior Prom is one of my lighter memories. I had a white satin dress trimmed with rhinestones. It came from Saks Fifth Avenue, and I knew it was right. I did not wear corduroy slacks under it. I wore Coty's Emeraude behind my ears and at other strategic points. Robert was there, but not, alas, as my escort. Nevertheless the young man who took me had his assets. Among them was a dress suit, so much more sophisticated than the usual tux that he was in great demand. The young lady who had invited Robert was a lifelong friend of mine, and I worked on her. I got to dance with Robert a good many times.

I have always considered that fabulous dress as the best investment of six months' allowance I have ever made. It convinced Robert that I was not entirely a hoyden.

The instructor of mathematics never saw it, I guess. At least he never changed his opinion of me. On the day when I received my bachelor's degree, the day when I knew more than I had ever known before or ever shall again, he stood behind Professor Fiske in the academic procession and chatted with a visiting potentate about the chapel steeple. After all he was only trying to make conversation, but he picked a terrible flub to make it with. He told a story, which had somehow become legend, of a day when I was supposed to have got stuck on that lofty spire, and added, for his own prestige, that he had directed me in the difficult matter of making the descent.

I guess Professor Fiske decided that at that point the public burning of my diploma could not possibly take place, so she turned on him like a tiger: "In the first place, if Mary had climbed that steeple, she would not have got stuck; and, in the second, if she had got stuck, she would have stayed there till she starved before she'd have let you get her down."

In any case nobody burned my diploma. In fact, I even got a fellowship in the graduate school, but, stall the inevitable hour as I would, it was during the thirties that I had to leave the ivied halls. And the thirties were no picnic for job hunters.

I think I was really frightened the day that I saw an old man picking over the garbage and rescuing bits of meat from the plate scrapings. Up to that moment hunger had been, like most things, an academic problem to me. From that point on I understood poverty and despair with my heart.

I was lucky. I landed a job growing orchids, and the irony of it struck me quite as forcibly as it will strike you. Bob was industrious and he landed one too. He worked on a drill boat, setting off dynamite to deepen a channel — not a cozy job, particularly in July, with a nice big crane reaching up into the sultry air for sparks of static or lightning.

My luck held. Robert asked me to marry him. I hope not as a simple calculation of the lesser of two evils! Our engagement was an occasion for a good deal of comment.

Mrs. Slaight held forth on my undeserved good fortune at some length in the butcher's shop. She was joined in her comments by several people, but, O Dr. Holland, with your Stradivarius that fiddled so often at Tongueslip, I hope you know how much it meant when your comment was relayed back through the Ladies' Aid: "There is much to be said for Robert's good fortune too! "

How often when I might have been short, or curt, or even unkind, I have remembered what you said and tried to deserve it!

YESTERDAY one of my friends remarked that my problems have always been purely intellectual. I wish she could have been about in the spring of 1938. One hesitates to cry crocodile tears, for as one grows older it becomes increasingly apparent that the best thing to do with heartaches is to keep quiet about them, lest the public, when one walks down the street, cross to the other side.

Dad was very ill, and not able to do many things that he should have done in the parish. There was a small progressive and practical element that was determined to get rid of him, and the chicanery to which it descended was incredible. The problem lay in the necessity of keeping him from discovering what was going on. We managed it, I think. Though he would never have told us had he known.

Mother was in bed with a broken hip. I was to be married in six weeks, and it was Mrs. Loder who saved the day. She lived next door at the time, and had the miraculous quality of being able to keep everything in order. Lists, people, things, fell into a neat pattern under her hand, and I don't know what I should have done without her. I was working, and it was essential that I continue to. Mrs. Loder and the Duchess and Mother Arny started in on the invitation lists.

Between the parish, the university, and a lifetime of living in the same town, we had amassed quite a number of friends. We checked the parish files, the college files, and the telephone book. It became obvious that the church would not hold all the people who should be invited.

Where, oh, where, to draw the line! Dear familiar problem to all brides! We finally solved it in a way that caused a minimum of hard feeling. The list remained at twelve hundred! Mrs. Loder sent the invitations, and the United States Post Office did a wonderful job — it lost half of them!

This posed a lovely problem, which may or may not have been intellectual. It seemed to me rather personal when my beloved friend Pauline, maid of honor and lady of complete discernment and tact, informed me that her parents had not been invited. It was equally complicated when I discovered that the dean of the university, and the chairman of the board of trustees had also been " lost in the mail "! There was only one way out. We put notices on all bulletin boards, explaining the loss of the invitations and declaring open house!

Then came the matter of the music. I like hymns at church services and wanted to find a suitable one. Mother Arny settled that by studying the lists, looking wryly at the hymnal, and suggesting " Ten Thousand Times Ten Thousand."

The day was almost upon us. The gifts were lined up in the middle room, and I was up to date on acknowledgements. Dad had a heart attack and was put to bed. With three days to go, it was impossible to postpone the wedding. A consultation of doctors was called. The young and inexperienced expert on cardiographs shook his head dourly. " Dr. Travis will not live out the week. For him to take the ceremony would be suicide."

Old Dr. Finnerty, a devout Roman Catholic, a man with an educated heart, shook his head. " To refuse him that right would be murder."

So, on June 25, 1938, at quarter of eight in the evening, I was lying on my bed, in satin slippers, a silver shilling in the right one, a blue garter, and a borrowed slip in their proper places. The Duchess hobbled in on crutches.

"My darling child, why aren't you dressed?"

"I'm waiting for my dress."

If Mother had been less of a Duchess, she would have blown her top. Instead she called Chloe, Chloe called the dressmaker, and the dressmaker called a cab. I had forgotten to tell that excellent lady the date of the wedding! Suppose she had been out! But she wasn't.

I made it! At two minutes of eight I came down the stairs better dressed than I ever had been or ever shall be.

The ushers had an enormous chair, under which they had put poles, and they lifted Dad into it to carry him to the church. Dr. Finnerty stood at the door holding it open. Dr. Lodge, the Episcopalian rector whom my father dearly loved, went behind him in vestments lest at the last minute Dad should feel unable to make the grade. As the poles went up on the ushers' shoulders, carrying my father in robes, hood, and prayer book, Dr. Finnerty grinned, "Don't let it go to your head!"

Meanwhile Bruce Johnson, the best man, and Robert, were pacing the vestry. At the first note of the wedding march I took my cousin's arm and he smiled down at me. At the same moment, in a wild dash as they went through the door, Bruce grabbed Robert's sleeve and ripped the price tag off his beautiful white dinner jacket!

It's funny the things one remembers. As we came down the aisle of that jam-packed church, Mr. Ross McElrath, a neighbor, leaned over and said, "Much happiness, Mrs. Arny."

He did better than Robert, who, when we arrived at the hotel in Lake George for our honeymoon, persisted in introducing me as "My wife, Miss Travis!"

Being independent and young, we decided to start our own household on our own terms. We were certain that we could meet any problem, alone and unassisted. The world was our oyster and we needed no advice.

We got ourselves an apartment, we each kept our car, and

we both kept our jobs. Such success and prosperity has seldom been the lot of the young. We got tired of one of the cars and bought a new sedan, we invested in a refrigerator, and we went to Bermuda. Not satisfied with these mundane matters, we had a baby, and from that time on life was a different matter altogether.

In the first place, when Tommy was born, I had an insight into Robert's calmness and self-control which, if it hadn't been so funny, would have turned me livid.

I put out my hand to shake him awake and told him to get the car, which he did, but not before he had asked me if he had time to shave. He shaved! I dare say that never before or since has a really tidy, poised, and restrained father had such a beautiful baby.

The world outside was not so calm and poised. It was trembling on the brink of disaster. While Tommy was coming into the world, the men who were trying to keep it together for him were lined up waist-deep in the water at Dunkirk waiting for the little boats, and other men, with blistered hands and under blistering fire, were rowing, paddling, driving outboards and cruisers, and even towing rafts across the English Channel.

Strangely, when I looked out the window I saw a funeral procession, with a caisson draped with a flag and foot soldiers following after. The doctor was standing at the foot of my bed watching it, and he looked suddenly very old and very tired. "Well, Mrs. Arny, they can kill them faster than you and I can make them live, I guess." He turned and walked out quickly, but not before I saw that he was afraid he would cry.

I looked at my son and hated war!

I was not educated to be a mother, and it is a matter of some concern and consternation to me that it is quite possible, in these United States, for a woman to possess a pile of sheepskins entitling her to all the privileges and rights thereto, a pile of sheepskins that would dress a pack of wolves in proper

67

garments, and still have no idea how to do a darn thing to a potato but boil it.

It is even more of a mystery to me how the female of the species can attain the status of a mother without even having been introduced to a washtub or a flatiron. But I did and, thank heaven for science, at least I knew how to sterilize a bottle, which is probably the only taught technique I possess that ever did me a bit of good. I can balance an equation, but, so help me Hannah, I can't balance a checkbook! I no longer try: we have a joint account.

And there are other attributes of the academic world that I seem to have absorbed along the way, the one usually mocked as absent-mindedness, which is in reality a kind of concentration on the abstract which makes you skin your chin on the concrete.

It was this concentration that proved my undoing. I was sitting on the very comfortable chair at the meat market, concentrating on a steak, when the Duchess walked in, her market basket over her arm and her cane tapping jauntily. Everyone in the place sprang to instant attention — that is everyone but me.

" Where," she asked, with the tone reserved for my particularly inane moments, " where is the baby? "

" Baby, what baby? "

" Thomas Travis Arny, your baby."

I was out of that shop like the proverbial bat and visualizing the apartment in flames and Tommy toasted to a crisp. I admit it — I had forgotten I had him. But all was well, and Tom was quite cheerful about the whole thing, having managed in my absence to get out of his play pen and into the jam cupboard. I never used to believe those pictures of gaumy little boys, but life was getting real now. The pictures are masterpieces of understatement.

That did it. And when Robert got home that night I told him what I had done. Since the day before I had tossed two

68

football tickets in the incinerator, thinking the Alumni Association envelope was just another "touch," my latest deficiency was not received with enthusiasm. Robert was courteous, as he always is, but he simply didn't believe me. I don't think he does yet, but he agreed that what we needed was a proper house where there was an apple tree and a fish pool and a hayloft. Then I would feel like a human being instead of life a cliff-dwelling mole, and perhaps be able to handle my job as wife and mother with the intelligence that those sheepskins had entitled him to expect. And if, by any chance, I threw out the tickets to the Wagnerian Ring, they would be in a garbage can, where there would be some hope of retrieving them. The incinerator was altogether too efficient.

We embarked on a house-hunting expedition. We looked at ranch houses, with their enormous picture windows, which seemed to me a subconscious expression of the fact that most of life was being lived in a showcase. We looked at contractors' houses, where on damp days no window would open and on dry days Tommy could watch the passing cars through the crack under the front door. We looked at country club estates where men, looking self-conscious in tall white hats, broiled steaks outdoors on charcoal grills, and at 1920 houses, where the first sound that greeted us on our early morning sojourn was that of the man next door brushing his teeth.

And then we looked at each other and went hand in hand to Tongueslip, asking admittance.

The small extra kitchen was adequate for my needs, and it was certain that Dad and the Duchess neither wanted nor could use nineteen rooms and five baths at once. It was equally certain that they *could* use the rent.

Our friends, prophets of gloom, shook their heads. No house, they swore, was big enough for two families, and to live with in-laws on both sides of us was unadulterated madness. We did not listen — people seldom do. The fact that Mother Arny is a genius at minding her own business made no difference to our friends, but it did to me, and I was quick to grasp the fact that with four doting grandparents on the job I should have no baby-sitter problems. We just heaved a sigh of relief, and wished we had a cat so that we could swing it in the wide open spaces between the apple trees, the fish pond, and the hayloft.

Tommy got splinters from the hay shoot, fell out of the apple tree, and into the fish pool — usually when trying to slide on ice that was too thin; but what is the use of trying to convey the situation inherent in the phrase " thin ice " to those who have never been doused in chilly water for their folly? It seems reasonable to assume that one reason for the apparent decline in the mores of the young, bewailed by Micah, Plato, and *The New York Times*, is that language is an adult affair, and its similes and clichés never quite catch up to the situations in which the young find themselves. Imagine abjuring a pilot in a ramjet not to fire until he sees the whites of their eyes!

[9]

WHERE were you on the afternoon of December 7, 1941? Were you listening to the Philharmonic? Or were you idly flipping through the funnies? Or were you, as we were, still at dinner?

It was a momentous occasion at Tongueslip because it was the Duchess' birthday. Chloe and I had taken great pains with the setting of the table. The silver shone; the glasses gleamed. The best Dresden china had been taken out for this festive dinner party, and the Satsuma cups and saucers stood ready on the coffee tray.

There were thirteen of us at the table, a fact that I tried to ignore, and we were twitting the Duchess because she was the only one who had not been born on a historic date.

Dad was born on the anniversary of Waterloo, Robert on Constitution Day. To be perfectly honest, I missed Columbus Day by three minutes, but I argued that that was pretty close, clocks being what they are.

Chloe set the coffee tray beside the Duchess and went out to the kitchen for the plates. There was a sudden thunderous knocking on the door and Ganz — trained from childhood to turn to the church in all crises — came into the dining room. "Herr Pastor, I think you should know — in my prowl car I heard it yet — the Japs have bombed us!"

Robert got up and turned on the radio. A few notes of achingly peaceful music came through the speaker and then:

"We interrupt this program to bring you a special news bulletin. The Japanese have attacked Pearl Harbor, Hawaii, by air, President Roosevelt has just announced. The attack was also made on all naval and military activities on the principal island of Oahu."

The beautiful plates hit the floor with a shattering crash. Ice cream dribbled across the Chinese rug and quenched the flame issuing from the mouth of the woven golden dragon.

Mother did not turn her head, but I knew that her heart ached for Chloe, with her two sons — that it hurt for the love, the courage, and the sacrifice that had seen them through college for this — and I saw her look at Mother Kate, whose eyes, filled with tears for the first and only time that I can remember, rested for a tender, bitter moment on the three tall young men she had borne and raised. I know that my own arms tightened, with the protective tightening of the jungle, around my baby, and something which does not belong at a civilized dining table, with its paper-thin varnish covering the jungle so carefully, surged through my body. All the little hairs on the back of my neck answered that challenge and stood up.

"Ganz," said the Duchess, "won't you sit down and have

71

some coffee; do break the curse of the thirteen!" She continued to pour into the Satsuma cups with a perfectly steady hand.

Robert got a cloth, wrung out in cold water, and wiped the ice cream off the rug.

I sat frozen and furious. "How can you all be so calm? How can you go on behaving as though nothing had happened? Can't you see that the world we have always lived in is at an end?"

Robert looked at me and I shrank like Alice after eating the wrong side of the toadstool! Mother spoke, and I wished I had eaten it all and were invisible.

"I have always found that in a crisis the best thing to do is to attend to the task at hand. How much sugar, Kate?"

I could have smacked them all because I knew they were right!

Dad put his spoon down slowly. "You know, I can't help wondering if this isn't one more example of the fatal weakness of Christianity. We always insist on the action applied with regard to the woman taken in adultery even when we are trying to cope with the money-changers in the Temple!"

Father Arny said, "Please elucidate!"

"It's the same queer psychology that we Americans always apply. I met a lot of it when I was inspector of prisons. Let a man be condemned to die and the great American public howls in pity for him; it never howls in pity for his victims. Why not? If a man has mental smallpox and twists every truth into some monstrous lie, we pity him but we never think of all the healthy minds he has tainted!

"We yell: 'Give him a chance'—'Let him go free'—'Let him who is without sin cast the first stone,' and we let him loose on society to wreak more damage and more tragedy. I do believe that there are people who, if they had demolishd every star in heaven but one, would sit calmly enthroned on the last bit of solid matter in the universe and demand the privilege of running that one on the basis that they had now learned from experience!"

Somebody said: "But, Dad, we are supposed to forgive. Really, if we were honestly Christians, we would forgive those poor beggars of Japs. They just don't know any better."

Dad hit the table with his fist and I shuddered for the rest of my china! "They do know what they are doing, as much as any of us ever knows what we are doing! If you'll *read* the words that Jesus said, and the things that Jesus *did* instead of listening to a lot of profound blather about what somebody who reads carelessly says He did, you will discover that He only counseled forgiveness when the hurt was to *Him* personally. That was His affair and He forgave, but He did not overlook what was done to others, to innocent people, to little children, and He made His position on those things exceedingly plain! Indeed, the devil quotes Scripture to his purpose and if we don't — I'm sorry, I've preached so many sermons I just go off on one naturally — Give me a cuppa, will you, Duchess?"

I've thought about that partial sermon a lot. I wish it had been finished!

Ganz ate his cake stolidly. The phone began to ring.

For the next five years it continued to ring, and only a few times was it with accurate information.

We had the open phone for this sector, which meant that all official information came over it and it was usable even in blackouts.

Monday it rang: "Enemy planes are reported converging on New York. All school children in this area are being sent home. Tune your radio to local short wave."

The school children came home all right, but a lot of mothers were not at home and a lot of front doors were locked. Over the next half hour we collected a crew that would have turned the Pied Piper's head.

They were pea green and sobbing. Some of them threw up

from sheer nerves. My Chinese rug took another beating!

Life at Tongueslip was definitely changed. The peaceful old world in which we had always moved was gone. Instead of drifting down a placid stream, we had to row up it. Robert's brothers, Malcolm and Vin, were called up. Robert tried to get into the Navy, for he said, " I can paint any part of a boat, and boy, can I make brass shine! "

Evidently radio tubes were considered more useful than paint and polish. The brass would have none of Robert. If the hours put in at the office were any indication, the Armed Forces of the United States, unlike those of Napoleon Bonaparte, traveled on radio tubes, not on their stomachs!

The rest of the United States was, you will remember, quite concerned over its stomach. Landlords pushed up rents, food prices soared, and when these were rolled back, it did not take the greedy few long to find the loopholes.

Aunt Mary was caught up in this maelstrom. Her landlord wanted her room. He could charge a new tenant a higher figure and he set out to make the old lady's position untenable. He turned down the heat, he turned off the hot water, he charged an extra fee for use of lights and radio.

At eighty-three one cannot cope with these things. There was no hope for betterment. Aunt Mary came to Tongueslip to get warm and she stayed.

She was Dad's oldest sister. Born in the little village of Gee Cross in Lancashire, she had gone to work in the cotton mills when she was eight. Her only schooling came from the Unitarian minister, who, so far as I can discover, was the one white hope of kindliness and education in that so limited life. It bothered Aunt Mary to her dying day that this poor benighted chap was most certainly in hell and roasting; he did not, of course, subscribe to the proper creed.

I tried to comfort her with the argument that surely heaven would hear *her* petitions, based as they were upon the proper credentials, and that I was sure that this good man occupied a pleasant mansion in a happy acre of heaven.

She would not be comforted. I suspect that in a way she rather enjoyed the fact that *she* was saved and the rest of us were in for it. Her certainty of damnation included us, and my cousins Gottlieb and Eva, who, in unending love and patience, bore the brunt of her most difficult years, loved her, cared for her, and sheltered her with their roof. Personally I am not called upon to worry about the Unitarian minister, Gottlieb, or Eva, for there are areas in which I heartily concur with my brethren of other faiths. One of these is that I am unalterably convinced that the souls of the righteous are in the hands of God.

Aunt Mary concentrated upon whatever she did or thought, to the exclusion of all else. Her bent shoulders, after seventy years away from it, still seemed to be trying to keep her keen blue eyes close to the threads of an enormous loom. Its ghost rode her still, and her thin, wiry body was still evidence of never, never enough to eat. Her gnarled fingers bespoke toil which kept her from the sun and earth except in darkness or on Sunday, and on Sunday she did nothing but breathe and did that very quietly.

Dear Aunt Mary — how she worried about all of our protestant souls and what exercise she gave them in the " contrary virtues " of liberality, temperance, and brotherly love!

But she mellowed as the years rolled, an achievement that very few attain when by reason of great strength the days of their years have passed fourscore.

Nor was Aunt Mary's advent the only invasion of Tongueslip. Three unoccupied bedrooms and a bath remained. In the age of committees this fact could not long go unnoted.

I had at the time of Pearl Harbor one and two thirds babies, two sets of grandparents, a very tired husband, and a Victorian aunt. This, the billeting organization felt, was not enough — I should take in some defense workers.

Their arguments that three extra people in the house would

not cause me any difficulties were completely logical and there wasn't a word of truth in them, but I have chaired committees, and so out of sisterly feeling I succumbed.

The first thing that happened was that one of the engineers tried to be helpful in a blackout. Robert was on duty outside and the young man was going around with a flashlight checking our blinds. I saw the light and thought he was in Tommy's room, miscalculated my position in the dark, and stepped right off the top of the stairs, down which I crashed ignominiously.

I was so surprised that I was completely relaxed, but I assure you that the family were horror-struck and terrified. It comforts me to know that the Creator designed expected babies to take bumps without damage. In an effort to propitiate the fates for the responsibility he felt, the young man ordered a bushel of oranges from Florida. These arrived on March 13, Saturday. I knew that I had little time to make the most of them. Sunday I got to work to make marmalade.

There was definite evidence that I had best not delay in the cooking, and at that moment two white-winged crossbills, not seen for years in New Jersey and never before seen by me, landed on the pine tree right outside the kitchen window!

I looked at the birds, looked at the oranges, and was again forcibly reminded that I'd better get along with the marmalade.

I just made it — just.

At twelve fifty I poured the last paraffin on the last jar, and at one twenty Mary Katharine expressed her opinion of the world she had precipitately entered with a contemptuous sneeze.

I often wonder at the intricate pattern of life, and how it links up completely unrelated episodes at the far corners of the earth.

How could I guess that the fact that I got no breakfast the day after Mary K. was born would years later save my life?

76

I was annoyed — there are times when one is very weary and annoyance becomes articulate. I aired my views. Just how I was supposed to feed a baby and survive myself without breakfast became for a while the central focus of my thinking.

When I have a good meal under my belt and eight hours sleep behind me, I can be really concerned about other people's problems even if they are a world away. Hungry and exhausted, I am selfish to an appalling degree. I didn't give the poor devils in Army and Navy hospitals a second thought. I wanted my boiled egg and considered it a personal insult that there was no nurse to give it to me.

The supervisor, with infinite patience, and a weariness much greater than mine, got me an egg — to my everlasting shame. It was this egg that was the means of my introduction to Mac.

Years afterward, when Tommy became bewitched with birds, I was visiting a friend in the hospital. The same supervisor was on duty, and she looked at me with austere starchiness and remarked, " Are you still as fond of eggs as ever? "

I cringed — expecting a blast. She continued: " Our new director might give you some information. I heard you mentioning your son's interest in birds. Her husband is an eminent ornithologist and they live near you."

So that was how I met Mac and that was how I got a sense of proportion when I learned that while I was yelling about the egg, Mac was director of nurses at the base hospital for Pacific casualties, where nobody was much concerned about anything less important than life; and that was how on a night, waist-deep in blizzard, there was a nurse who cared enough about me to wade through it and turn on the oxygen which kept the breath of life in me.

[10]

I WISH I could somehow invite you to a birthday party at Tongueslip. If you could just be here and we could meet you, and show you around and visit, it would be so much more fun.

You would come in through the garden walk, at this time of year bordered with cottage tulips and honest-to-goodness daffydowndillys, the big fluffy kind. You would walk under the apple tree, the lovely Red Astrachan whose blossoms now fill the air with fragrance. The bees are working it and there is a hum of industry in its gnarled branches. You would pass the wall and see the new ferns just pushing up their fiddle-heads, and the moss so soft and green between the flagstones.

At the front door you would stretch out your hand and shake the old silver sleigh bells which hang on a strap of harness beside the knob, and our beloved Chloe would open the door to you and ask you to come in and rest yourself while she found " Miss Mary." Perhaps you'd notice the portrait of me as a bride, but I doubt if you would connect it when you saw me. My hair is gray now, and worn in braids over my head. I like to think I am still slim and elegantly tall, but the scales betray me at an imperfect 136.

You would sit in the big wing chair looking around you at all the unrelated things in the room, and when I put out my hand to welcome you, you would ask about the big stone fireplace.

Then Chloe would tell you that we set great store by those andirons, that she keeps them shining like gold because they are all that is left of the wilderness home where my great-grandmother was killed by the Indians.

You would look at the old pine corner cupboard, and I would take down the little blue pottery figure that a Moslem friend of ours excavated from Tutankhamen's grave, and the

78

old Greek urn that was given to some young man hundreds of years ago as a prize for the discus throw in the original Olympic games.

If you seemed really interested in old things, and did not evidence signs of suspecting our sanity, someone would surely take out the old goblet, now flaky and iridescent as glass long buried always is. We would tell you that its presence is the essence of our household, for the same friend who dug in Egypt and gave us the little figure, also dug in Palestine, and he found that goblet in a house in Nazareth, together with the fragments of an aged carpenter's plane, and we always hope and dream that perhaps it was *the* house, the house in all the world where we would have wanted to be friends and guests.

Then Chloe would ask where you were to sit at table and you would join us at the long harvest trestle in the Pine Room. You would see the books, thousands of them, reaching to the ceiling, every conceivable thing from the old *Bay Psalm Book,* one of the earliest American publications, to the current *Radio Amateur's Handbook.* You would smell the old leather and the scent of sassafras logs burning on the hearth, and you would join in a simple meal, selected by the one whose birth-day it was.

I guess at this time of year it could be Mary Katharine's, and you would be asked to sit beside her. She is tiny and slight like the Duchess, with big blue eyes over which she has astounding control. It might surprise you a little to have the person on each side of you take your hand, but you would know right away that you were becoming part of a tradition so old that we do not know where it originated, and you would bow your head, and if you looked as though you would understand, you would be asked to say grace for us. If it was obvious that you might not know a blessing, one of the children would receive the secret sign from Robert and would save you the possibility of embarrassment. Polly would watch you surreptitiously and all you would see would be the top of her honey-colored hair, and Tom would twinkle with a becoming mixture of mirth and sobriety.

This is Mary Katharine's birthday, remember. So we would have chicken broth, served from an aged silver tureen which sadly needs plating. This would be followed by roast beef, of which she would get the first slice and a big crisp piece of fat. Mashed potatoes, gravy, green beans, and pears stuffed with cottage cheese would follow. Then Grandmother Arny would go out to the kitchen to light the candles while the children cleared the table for Chloe. Grandmother Arny always makes the birthday cakes. Mary K.'s would be the "fruit kind," with citron and nuts and maraschino cherries and bits of dates. It would be surrounded with sweetheart roses and on top of it would be candles in little holders shaped like birds. Chloe would carry it in with the candles twinkling in the dark, for Tommy would have turned off the lights, and we would all sing, "Happy Birthday."

If by a miracle everyone was home, or within reasonable reach, it would swell to quite a chorus. Robert's baritone would hold to the melody and Malcolm, his brother, would harmonize. Dad would whistle a rich warbling trill; Vin, Robert's younger brother, would pantomime, and Mary K. and Polly would try to keep singing without laughing. Tommy is sure of his notes now and has a nice reliable tenor. The grandmothers, Aunty Fern, and Aunt Mary, lend a fragile quality to the song, but there is no quaver; my own contralto is passable, and Chloe has a rich melodious eighth-note harmony which I would give my eyeteeth to possess. We might sing the song three times with variations just because we love to sing, and by that time the candles would be dripping on the icing, and Mary K. would puff out her cheeks and blow.

While she cut the cake, you would be served ice cream, probably peach, in the Chinese bowls, and the eternal argument would begin. You would be asked to decide whether they are blue or green. No matter what you said, half the family would contradict you, and the question would remain undecided, as it has done now for years.

While the grownups had their coffee, which would be properly poured from a silver pot and then refilled from the aluminum jug, lugged in from the kitchen by whoever wanted seconds first, Mary K. would open her presents.

Only one of these is definitely foreseeable. She will get a baby doll and it will have a bottle of perfume in some odd kind of container in its arms. Mary K. collects baby dolls and perfume bottles. At the end of each chronological year the pile of defunct infants in the armchair grows deeper, but even those that have no heads are so deeply beloved that they cannot be disposed of. The little perfume bottles are neatly arrayed on a shelf and protected from loss and breakage by the Duchess, who, I think, encouraged the habit as an extension of her own mania for jade snuffbottles.

After dinner we would play charades, and if it were Friday, we would watch " Mama " on the television set. Somebody would read a story aloud, Vin and Tommy would retire to the attic to tinker with the short wave radio, Malcolm and Robert would get off on some argument and express their opinions with identical gestures and *moues*. Aunty Fern and Aunt Mary would go into a huddle over last week's sermon, Dad would light his pipe and perhaps play a tune or two on his concertina, which if it were liked would be sung by the assembled company, and, otherwise, would be ignored. Grandmother Arny, the Duchess, and I would ask you if you played bridge, and pray silently that you would say you loathed it.

Somebody would wake up to the fact that it was getting on to eight thirty and go out and give a hand in the kitchen. Whoever that lucky someone was would undoubtedly learn something from Chloe she had never known before, and would not have the slightest idea that she had absorbed it until some crisis arose in life, when it would suddenly swim to the top of her conscious mind and present the kindly, reasonable answer to the problem.

Eventually bedtime would come and the children would disappear. There would be the sound of the shower running, and a few altercations about who should have the bath tub first, and where is the toothpaste — and then there would be silence.

Somebody would drop a belligerent dogma into the calm pool of polite conversation and everybody but you would know that the speaker didn't believe a word of it. If you were quick of tongue, you might be able to get a word in edgewise, and if you could twist a phrase to slide through some chink of pedantry on the part of one of us, you would be loved forever.

If it became perfectly apparent that you were convinced that we were all furious and insane, someone would come to your rescue, and the topic would disappear as if by magic, giving place to your favorite book, opera, play, or hobby; a tray of Coke, ice water, lager, and other accouterments would appear, and disappear, and at the end of the evening you would be taken to your destination by whoever happened to have piled his car into the barn last. This because nobody else could get his out.

You would leave in one of two states, either completely exhausted and determined never to darken the door of Tongueslip again or eager to come back the next morning to pound out the things that remained to be settled from last night's argument. If you were in this latter class, you would be warmly welcomed.

The Duchess would take you into the garden and fill your arms with daffodils, someone would undoubtedly offer you either a perfectly fascinating caterpillar which you could take home and watch, or a frog, or, if you were exceedingly popular with the children, you might even merit a garter snake.

You would be expected to bring in a piece of sassafras wood as you passed the woodpile, or remove the stray bit of chickweed which you detected in the rose bed. If you did these things without prompting, we would have that warm delicious feeling in our ears and finger tips which means, we have struck treasure, we have a new friend, for it is our friends, with their new and different horizons, who are constantly opening the doors to adventure.

Sometimes they get us into things which take us out over our heads, literally.

It was a man we met at the Audubon dinner who fired the spark of curiosity that took us to Bermuda. He told us about the wonders under the sea and showed us pictures he had taken with a homemade underwater camera.

Some people feel that if they see travelogues and watch television they have absorbed the thrill of travel. To me the feel, the smell, the little sounds which no microphone picks up are the essential ingredients in experience. How can one really savor life from an armchair? Intellectual absorption of an experience is a far cry from having had it.

Life — thank God — is often difficult and trying! So many people complain bitterly of the injustice of fate in selecting them to undergo hardship, privation, and sorrow. Perhaps they just don't realize how lucky they are. I can think of nothing more terrible than to have walked through life and never really tasted it. Perhaps this is because of a philosophy evolved after years of trying to make sense of the vagaries of the pilgrimage upon which we are all mutually embarked.

I think I have found one answer to it all. At least it is an answer for me. If we are to get anywhere in life — and by " we " I mean mankind — we must be always moving forward toward some distant and unseen goal.

Some people can just sit life out, but some people have to go ahead through the wilderness and mark the trail. These are the ones who take the blows, sorrow, pain, disappointment,

83

despair. And there is a reason for it. A good reason.

The strong must mark the road for the weak, and the weak then, seeing that it can be done, gain faith to follow. Thus life expands for all men at what seems to be the expense of the courageous. But the richness lies in the fact that those who follow on unscathed never, never taste the heady wine of living, for life is a covenant with God and must be seasoned with the salt of sorrow if it is to have full savor.

If one wants the view from the top, one must climb and be weary. If one stays forever in the valley for comfort's sake, one can never see the distant city.

This is the premium for strength, the balm for wounds, the sustenance against blows, that passing through the valley of weeping one may make it a well.

There are adventures and adventures, some hard, some easy, but one of the most breath-taking of all journeys is the journey under the surface of the mother of life — the sea. Those who know the sea and her moods both love and fear her. Robert and I have for the wide blue sweep an intimate affection, born of a day when the knowledge of the life beneath her inscrutable exterior became a part of us. Down in the tropics where the man-of-war birds glide on tireless wings, where the little coral atolls are swept by fierce seas, where all life is a blaze of color and song and light, the ocean is filled with living jewels which can only be seen in its depths.

It was not easy to find someone who could help us with diving equipment, and each time we asked we were met by blank stares. The tourist is supposed to search for nothing more unusual than rum swizzles. Finally an ancient native, almost as venerable as the twisted cedar under which he lay somnolently munching a mango, told us whom to see, but he too looked after us in amazement, shaking his head in lethargic surprise.

There was no line-up at the diving helmet bar, no competition whatever. Various casual instructions concerning the danger of snarled hoses were given us, and the owner of the dilapidated impedimenta started the compressor which squeaked at every stroke.

We wore dark bathing suits and sneakers to reduce our resemblance to bait, and as we stepped to the diving ladder I looked at the sea, blue and clear, and at the purple shadows which marked the location of the reef.

Robert smiled his slow, easy smile. "Well, there it is; if you want to see it, you'll have to go down and look." Visions of octopuses as big as a whale drifted through my mind. I drew a deep breath and decided to go under before I scared myself to death.

The air gushed into the helmets as we took our first plunge. Bubbles rose in an even stream as we descended. The regularity of the pulsing pump was reassuring, but one couldn't help wondering why people have such sublime confidence in their fellow men. If this chappie should stop pumping we would drown; but on the other hand if the bus driver or the engineer, or the driver coming the other way, stops thinking, you will be smashed to a pulp. I never heard of anybody drowning in a helmet, but I've heard of lots of traffic accidents . . . forget it and look around!

Down, down, down, hand over hand on the rusty chain, till our feet touched gently on the pink sand of the bottom. We bounced like balloons and were suddenly aware that the sixty-pound helmets no longer had any weight. As we looked up, the surface of the water was a sheet of pure silver, hammered by the ripples, impenetrable. This was the looking-glass world. Only the black air line cutting the surface connected us with the earth on which we had always lived.

Robert looked around slowly. We could not communicate with words, but I knew from experience that he would take with him an accurate and indelible picture of everything he saw. He gesticulated in slow motion and I realized that he was pointing to a cliff of coral on our right. Though the water seemed perfectly clear, it was as though we were inclosed in a sphere, beyond which loomed weird shapes and strange creatures seen through a green and ever-densening fog.

We worked our way toward the cliff and learned in short order to watch the waving sea fans which indicated the presence of strong currents. These streams of rushing water cannot be seen, but they catch one off guard and tumble one to the bottom with the suddenness of a flying tackle.

Long fronds of fabulously scarlet seaweed drifted across our path. Parrot fish glided through the water within easy reach. We pushed aside an enormous and rather awesome fish which I took to be a grouper. It looked a little dejected — if you can imagine a dejected fish — and I for one felt ashamed for my rudeness. After all, we were the intruders. Hundreds of tiny fish maneuvered past the glass through which we viewed them. Blue, scarlet, lemon yellow, and some fluorescent and striped in fantastic patterns, they flowed in infinite variety. Some were curious and gawked in our faces; others went about their business with schooled precision. Swarms of small creatures that resembled neon signs floated into view and I patted an enormous angelfish which loafed into reach.

Something was bothering Robert. He kept looking at the bottom and feeling carefully with his feet. Later I discovered that he was afraid that he would tread on a sea pudding, but at the time I thought he was watching the pearl oysters which, lined with lovely blue, snapped closed at our approach.

In the eery half-light under the cliff I kept a sharp eye out for barracuda. Just what I thought I should do if one appeared I do not know. They move like greased lightning and are lethal. A sea bat flapped slowly along the bottom, looking like a prehistoric bird and making it apparent by its leisurely progress that it had all eternity to find a clam. I laughed aloud and my laughter racketed about in the confines of the helmet like the scream of a maniac in Bedlam. After that I was silent.

The reef proper was covered with pale rose and lavender

colonial hydroids about six inches high and resembling lilies of the valley blown from the thinnest glass. Dainty and fragile beyond belief, they were everywhere in a profusion like that of harebells in a mountain meadow, and exotic sponges formed a background of antediluvian splendor.

An unwary spiny lobster poked his feelers out of a deep cranny in the rocks and I grabbed him. These are creatures of the night and one seldom gets a good view of them. One wonders why a kind Providence lets naturalists get away with so much. There could just as well have been a moray eel in that hole, but there wasn't. It is strange to me that I can work up a dither over the hazards of week-end traffic, but when I am in the hands of nature it never occurs to me to be hagridden.

Four fathoms down one is as separated from a companion as though all eternity rolled between. Though the currents of water are clear and invisible, they, like the currents of life, form a barrier through which no understanding can truly reach. In the sea, as in life, one is alone. But as we came full circle to the rusty chain, there was a strange reluctance to leave this looking-glass world, the same reluctance that one desperately ill feels at the thought of approaching death. One pauses to look back, to wonder what might have been had one known more, understood better, been able to share one's understanding.

And then a strong hand reaches down through the surface, and the waters of the sea rush into one's face, one struggles for a moment, sees a new world, and hears a voice asking: "Well, how did you like it down there? Learn anything new?"

[11]

IT WAS not at all difficult for us to adapt ourselves to the looking-glass world at the bottom of the sea. There all was following the laws of nature, all was as it should be. But in the brave new world of the Four Freedoms I must have been a terrible anachronism. There is a fifth freedom which I seek for myself and my family, freedom of action, for I submit that any animal in the zoo can be free from fear and want, can say what it pleases, and hold to its own convictions. To be truly free a man must be free to *do* what he wishes, and what he wishes to do is the measure of the man.

Also I must be a dreadful coward, because during the days of World War II there was a long period when I was not free from fear. Perhaps it goes back to the period in 1918 when Dad was involved in the investigation of atrocities. The horror of war dwells much more in my heart than its glory. My nationalistic pride is further humbled when I consider the stories I heard from a friend who was a staff officer at the liberation of Buchenwald, and Dr. Mayo's recent remarks before the Security Council in which he points out the fact that there is something more durable in the spirit of man than in the reflexes of Pavlov. I am afraid of war and its bestiality and I admit it.

The afternoon when the four sons of the chief air raid warden were at our house helping with the banding of birds did not add to my peace of mind. "What," they asked, "are we going to do if our home is bombed?"

I made a desperate effort to be calm and casual. "Why, go to your shelter, sit it out, and hope for the best like the rest of us."

"We haven't a shelter. Dad has been too busy at meetings to make one; besides, Mom is on the emergency gang. She'll be out and we'll be alone."

That cheering aspect of the situation had not struck me before, and it seems that it hadn't struck anybody else either. When I pointed it out at a C.D. meeting I was immediately appointed to set up a series of neighborhood shelters for the children of C.D. workers.

The engineers came to look our shelter over, and to my utter amazement told me that the cellar of Tongueslip was, to their way of thinking, the safest place in town. "It's really built; that stone wall should stand up against anything we have in the way of bombs." Well, maybe so, but could I stand up against a crew of panicked children left in their most desperate hour by a uniform-crazy bunch of parents who wanted excitement at any price?

So far as I was concerned, World War II held no glamour. It was a war of nerves, purely and simply. A thousand petty frustrations and irritations piled one upon the other until tempers were raw with friction and judgment curdled.

The sirens were exactly the right pitch to set the dogs and the children screaming, not from fear but from discomfort to their ears. Most of the wardens were kind and courteous, but there were a few who had achieved power for the first time and took it out in the picayune. One would have thought they expected a submarine attack from the way they roared over cracks at the bottom of a blind under a porch. Once in the blackout I was caught out, about fifty yards from Tongueslip and a hundred from a shelter. The warden ordered me to the shelter and I ran for Tongueslip. That cost me a pretty bawling out in "court." I did not enjoy the knowledge of the strategic position in which I was sitting, triangled between New York, Patterson, and Newark, and I enjoyed even less being called to order by a warden who had not taken care of the necessities of his own household. I simmered to a slow boil when we had a party for the crew and they filtered out elsewhere to get enough liquor to make them immoderately tight. There are few things less useful than a very drunk man with an ego which was inflated to start with. I am sorry for the chief who had to cope with these psychological Nazis.

Perhaps my courage was not enhanced by the fact that I was about to present the United States of America with another citizen. Perhaps my annoyance with beautiful uniforms was due to the fact that I could not possibly have worn one had I had it. But I remember one night when the sirens started screaming with particular vividness.

I started up the stairs to follow the prescribed routine when Dad called me. " Come out here, will you please? "

I went, reluctantly.

The sky glow from New York was gone. The night was pitch-black, and the hoarfrost shimmered on the leaves. I shivered, but not from cold.

" Mary," Dad put his coat around me, " Mary, do you see any searchlights? "

" No."

" Do you hear any gunfire? "

" No."

" Well, if Hitler meant business, do you think for one minute that the night would be calm and quiet as it is? If there were planes within a hundred miles of us the searchlights would be reaching for them, and there would be antiaircraft fire. Stop shivering, child, and take advantage of a rare moment. Listen."

I stood still. Not a sound broke the quiet of the night. Not a light shone out in the darkness. No car hummed down the street. The leaves stirred, and a light breeze scuttled the fallen pine needles.

" Look up, Mary, look up! When it is dark like this you can see the stars."

" It's not for me, Dad, that I am so afraid. It's for the kids. To have the thought that they might have to live in a world where nothing matters but to survive."

"Then teach them so that they can survive, and give them something to survive for."

"But they are only babies. They couldn't last a week."

"I think they could. There is such a thing in the world as love, you know. Or had you forgotten?"

It was hard to remember love in a world where thirty-five thousand men had started the long march of Bataan. It was hard to understand love in a world where expediency was paramount, where at the flick of a switch a bloody dictator could be gilded into "our dear ally," where our oldest friends could turn their guns on our ships that came to fight their oldest enemy.

Love — what is love in a world gone mad?

It was the blood of my neighbor dripping into my veins and bringing me up out of blackness when Polly was born. It was the arms of the men on Bataan, exhausted and dying, carrying their weary brothers. It was the untold thousand little loyalties, the unnamed hundreds who hid our men on the River Line. It was the twelve silent hostages dying in a muddy field. It was the anguished silence of men under torture.

It was the people of Germany and Russia, and Japan and Italy, who did what they could for their country and for their men. Make no mistake about it — the little people are the same all over the world, and in the end they will win out over the men who plot wars for their own aggrandizement, the men who make shoddy gun barrels, the men who run the black market, the men who sell their friends for a loaf of bread, and already in the year 1942 there was a great seething and a great unrest.

Tom, Dick, and Harry were lying dead on the desert, in the jungle and on the tundra, but John and James and Joe were seeing the world which would otherwise have lain far beyond their narrow horizons.

John, James, and Joe would not soon forget the blind babies of Egypt, the gaunt skeletons of children dying on the

Bund at Shanghai while the world walked past, the Jews in the ghettos, and the untouchables in Bombay. John, James and GI Joe were beginning to learn about love too.

But not all of a sudden, not overnight. There is still the fellow who sits and shoots over a baited blind and tosses his cigarette into the dry weeds. A spiral of smoke curls up into the autumn sky and the phones begin to ring. " There's a fire at Glen Gray and it's creeping pretty close to the Scout camp. Will you come and give a hand? "

A lot of people had other pressing engagements, at bridge, at the beauty parlor, at the club, but a lot more didn't.

Robert drove the old Ford up the narrow track in the valley. Smoke billowed across the whole mountain, scorching, choking, blinding. Here and there sparks leaped the trail from crown to crown in the pines, and a roar would be followed by an explosion from the sap in the trunk and flaming torches would fall on the roadbed. Those who saw them stamped out the fire with their feet and dragged the branches out of the way.

We left the car by the lake, dragged shovels and burlap bags from the rumble seat, and I started to run.

Robert put out his hand. " Don't fall flat on your face in the first fifty yards of a mile run, Sugar."

I slowed to a walk.

The cabins of the Scout camp, built by generations of boys and men, stared across the woods, their window eyes gaping in fear. The flames crept through the underbrush nearer and nearer. Little licking tongues of flame kissed a dry leaf, consumed it, and with profligate passion went on to its neighbor. The woods were dry, so dry that the dust and ashes blew in a fine penetrating powder into our nostrils and our mouths. Blackened trees stood stark and smouldering. Men, women, boys, girls, sweat-sodden and sooty, flogged the advancing fire with soaking bags in endless rhythm.

Children so small that they had to double up to lug them,

carried buckets of water, and a woman from a nearby farm, wearing a fantastic brown sunbonnet and long skirts, swayed tirelessly between her dungaree-clad sisters and the lake, bearing buckets on a yoke across her shoulders.

The wind sprang up and the line of fighters wavered, but did not break. The Red Cross Canteen Corps was there with sandwiches and coffee. A steady stream of nourishment poured into aching muscles which stood out on bare backs. Shirts were a disadvantage, sparks clung to them.

Shovels clanged on rock, digging fire breaks, and suddenly a doe, with twin fawns, leaped between the tired men and women. Panic, heat, and smoke had driven her into the midst of her enemies. No one offered her harm. She stood absolutely still, her nostrils wide, and then walked slowly to the shore and drank quietly among the bustling water carriers.

Rabbits darted out of the underbrush, flocks of jays went over, screaming imprecations. The circle of fire narrowed. The distance to the cabins decreased.

For three days and nights, we, and our neighbors, fought that fire. It was a blessed release to have something tangible to battle. For three days and nights the fire moved inexorably closer to the cabins.

Fire hoses, which had been brought in, began to crumble from the sustained pressure. People began to crumble too, but always there was a line of swinging shoulders, and finally the fire was quenched.

There weren't any spectacular heroes at the fire. They were just our neighbors, fighting to save a dream and a memory. But when I saw the line of tired friends, leaning on shovels, sitting on logs, bathing their sooty faces in the pond, and smiling, something happened to me that was good. Good for the bottom of my heart. And when next day I saw blue dungarees, clean and mended, flying like banners of victory from the clothesline all around Tongueslip, all of a sudden, just like that, I wasn't afraid for my children any more. I stopped shaking inside. The sirens never gave me the "gleeps" again. I had met our neighbors.

After that Ten Ton Tillie, who was always the "victim" of First Aid, didn't strike me funny any more. I guess Teddy Mac-Lachen always picked her on the theory that if we could turn her over and give her artificial respiration, we could turn anything. What that man put into us and got out of us was something for any book.

I remember what a time the ladies had to learn to tie a square knot. Teddy had his fill of it, but was always perfectly courteous and patient. One day he had a stroke of genius. He went around looking at all the triangular bandages put together with granny knots, and he grabbed the ends and pulled as hard as he could. Then he handed them to their perpetrators and said, "Untie it please." A hundred beautifully manicured fingernails were ripped to the quick. The "ladies" understood perfectly. The next day they could all tie square knots. Tommy showed me how.

We had weekly tests under Ted's direction. A catastrophe was supposed to have occurred, and each "victim" was neatly labeled with a sign which stated categorically the nature of the injury. We were to fix it. The first such incident was a debacle. Ted sat rocking in despair with his head in his hands. "Mrs. Arny, call a hearse; call six hearses." I looked at him in dismay. Why?"

"They're all dead. You punctured the lungs of the one with broken ribs, you compounded the fracture of the right leg, you put the tourniquet on the right arm while the left arm bled the patient to death, and you gave morphine to somebody who was unconscious already."

Well, so I had. And lucky I did it there. We'd know better next time, all of us. And there was a next time. Only the patients weren't all neatly labeled. There was no semblance of neatness about it.

A wooden-topped station wagon from the Orthopedic Hospital's country home was trying to save time by carrying the garbage to the dump, and the ambulatory patients to the beach, at sixty-five miles an hour. Just as we came over the crest of the hill it hit a bump, turned over three times, and skidded into the ditch.

Robert turned our car into a field so that the children would not see the shambles, grabbed the blanket and the first-aid kit, and bolted down the hill.

Eight people were strewn along the highway amid glass, garbage, splintered wood, and gore. There were no neat signs on any of them, only blood surging rhythmically from heads laid open to the skull, twisted legs, faces unrecognizable as human, and utter silence.

Someone appeared from nowhere, took one look, and ran for a phone. Robert took the worst wound; I took the next. Hands were stretched out to us with ripped shirts and petticoats made into bandages. Thermos jugs of cold water appeared at our sides. Men stood in line to form a shade for the injured, and the blood ran against my shoes and dammed up and flowed over, but the surging stopped. It seemed to me hours that we worked alone. It must have been about fifteen minutes really.

The emergency squad arrived and felt carefully along bodies. The doctor lifted closed lids and watched to see if the iris would contract. Robert rolled blankets to make stretchers, and strong hands lifted the injured into farm trucks when the ambulance had left with the most critically injured.

Somebody said: "Better turn the truck over. The driver could be under it." Suddenly I couldn't bear it. "Robert, take me out of here. If there's another under that mess, I don't want to know it."

"There isn't, darlin'. I looked first thing. It's all right."

I remember one girl with a hauntingly lovely face, and I remember my fury at a fate which would toss these people, already the bearers of so many scars, into still another battle for life and health. A boy shook my arm. "What about that colored woman? Do you think she will live?" I looked at my hands and feet; the blood upon them was all the same color. If the woman was white or black, red or yellow, I hadn't noticed it.

Then I knew that Teddy had taught us more than the contents of the little gray book with the red cross on the cover. He had taught us concern for life, and that all men are brothers. For that, I am eternally grateful.

⌞12⌟

SOMETIMES I wonder about a passionate addiction to a world-wide sense of responsibility. The chief warden had one and didn't build a shelter for his own children. The shoemaker's children are proverbially unshod, and volumes could be written about psychiatrists who commit suicide, divorced marriage counselors, and cookbook authors whose husbands subsist upon bicarbonate of soda!

It just doesn't make much sense, any of it. One of the best Sunday school superintendents I ever knew taught his children to count with a deck of cards, and was an intimate friend of Mr. Barleycorn. Maybe it all boils down to the fact that "the race is not to the swift, nor the battle to the strong, . . . but time and chance happen to them all."

I know they do at Tongueslip. If they hadn't, you could add to the long list of flops at their profession the children of schoolteachers and the progeny of the clergy.

To put it mildly, Tommy was getting numerous. He did what he pleased, when he pleased, how he pleased. With two small babies and a little boy, I had my hands full. My education in the matter of rearing children was now complete; I had read all the books and was thoroughly conversant with the *ne plus ultra* of scientific child-raising. I was also, so my physician informed me, a candidate for that disease, rare among women, stomach ulcers.

No one ever got a hot meal at noon. Between cajoling from grandparents and stony indifference from me, the soup was always cold, the sandwiches were always dried up, and the dessert was always soggy. Refusal to eat infuriates Robert, and dinner was a pitched battle seven days a week, with the children always emerging victorious and the evening holding no promise of abatement.

On one never-to-be-forgotten Sunday the lid of my restraint was jiggling up and down like Watt's teakettle cover. I followed the procedure that has so often been my salvation. I got up and walked out, but before I went I set Mary Katharine in the middle of the floor and turned sternly to Tommy.

" If she yells there's going to be trouble for you, so see that you don't start anything! "

I closed the door firmly, determined to take my irritation into the garden and expend my energy profitably. When I am angry I am very apt to say things I don't mean, and experience has taught me that blowing off steam in private is safer than creating a scene.

Hardly had I reached the top of the garden path when Mary K. began to howl. I stormed back into the Pine Room ready to shellac Tommy. He was sitting obviously and completely innocent in the chair where I had left him, watching the screaming Mary K. with horror.

Light dawned!

That tiny vixen in the middle of the floor *wanted* me to yell at Tommy and cuddle her. She was really in the middle. Tommy could go and come as he pleased. Polly was the baby and everybody googled at her. Mary K. wanted some excitement and had worked out a method of getting it. I looked at

97

my offspring and suddenly got wise to myself.

I was well on the way to becoming a disgracefully bad parent.

We had read all the books, and had been puzzled at the time about *when* children become old enough to have manners and consideration inculcated, but had been sure that the experts knew what they were talking about when they said, "A child must be shown what is right by example and led, not forced, into doing it." How was I to "lead" Mary K. into not tormenting Tommy and outsmarting me into blaming him?

We put some rather solid thought upon the matter. Looking at it from the point of view of the elder members of the family, we saw trouble ahead. Looking at it from our own point of view, we saw nothing but problems. It seemed suddenly clear that if three generations of people were going to live in the same house with a modicum of peace, either everybody had to "express himself" or everybody had to be at least decently considerate.

A week end I had once spent in the country came vividly to mind; I conjured up the most dreadful three days of my life. Bathing suits were all over the stairs, so that descent became a matter of care or disaster; everyone was fighting over who should have the car; my hostess was screaming: "I've told you a hundred times to get rid of that cat! Look what she's done now — eaten all the crabs!" (I eventually discovered that they had had the cat for eight years and that she always ate the crabs.) People, male and female, stalked into my bedroom in every state of dishabille including the ultimate, and pawed through drawers looking for things that could never be found and then other people said to me at the Beach Club, "Such a charming family — so free from inhibitions!"

No, so help me, no — the books were doubtless right — but inhibitions, repressions, and psychoses to the contrary notwithstanding, I could not and would not bear a lifetime of cats, crabs, fights, altercations, and wet bathing suits! I smacked Mary Katharine on her little pink behind, scooped the latest book on child psychology off the table, and jammed it into the garbage can.

A wonderful sense of emancipation swept over me. I could breathe!

The next time Tommy put his foot over the curb into Watchung Avenue I did not reason with him sweetly about the danger of trucks, I clouted him, much more gently than the truck would have. He never dangled his feet in the gutter again!

When Polly started to dismantle the shelves of the Acme, I removed her and let her sit and yell in the gocart while I did my shopping in peace.

When Mary Katharine did what she always did with oatmeal — tipped up the bowl and poured it over her head — I let her sit in her high chair while the starchy brew solidified on her face and hair. Then after I, for the first time in years, had had my soup hot, my sandwiches not dried out, and a second cup of tea, I put her in the bathtub and told her to get the oatmeal off herself.

This attitude I have preserved fairly consistently from that day to this. Summed up it is: If you are impossible you may take the consequences.

Probably our children will grow up with terrible inhibitions — I hope so. I can think of nothing more desirable than children whose psychoses prevent them from writing four-letter Anglo-Saxon words on the back fences of life. Also, I think it highly unlikely that I personally will get ulcers of the stomach.

" Peace! It's wonderful! "

Little by little I found our children being counted in instead of out. Their popularity grew by leaps and bounds. Tommy was constantly invited to the zoo and the museum; Mary K. was taken to the circus, and my neighbors did not seem so reluctant to keep an eye on Polly for me. I was emancipated. I could actually go out for an afternoon. Mother, Dad, and Mother Arny and Aunty Fern were perfectly willing to take care of my offspring while I made a quick trip to Boonton Reservoir to watch shore birds. Life lost its nightmare quality and took on some of the aspects of a soap opera!

Sooner or later the bête noire of Tongueslip will have to be mentioned. I'm going to take care of that now because our child experts will undoubtedly scream: " See! We told you. They may have manners, but they've got allergies as a result."

To which I shall reply, " Nuts." Dad is allergic to pork — one bite and he is purple-spotted. Mother is allergic to veal — it swells her up as though she'd been in a hornet's nest. I am allergic to coffee — one cup of coffee and I see cars going off cliffs and my children being tattooed with concentration-camp numbers.

All the Arnys are allergic too, so I think Mendel's law has a lot more to do with it than Freud's successors.

Allergies however *do* present a problem. Tom can't eat wheat, cheese, spinach (which he perversely loves), beets, potatoes, beans, chocolate, bananas, and fifteen or twenty other items. When he gets into the army, the Quartermaster's Corps will love him. One slice of toast and he is in bed with a fever.

Mary K. and Polly have the same peculiarity. Mary K. folds up in shock if she touches grapefruit, and goes into asthma over apples, cider, or vinegar. All these things can be avoided, but I was glad when the horsehair pew cushions were taken out of the church. Every high festival of Christendom is no longer followed by a week of croup kettles at Tongueslip.

To satisfy allergy, palate, and budget in those days of rationing and shortage presented its problems, and we were determined to find a reasonable out.

Our first step toward one acre and independence was the installation of chickens at Tongueslip. Our enlightened town has an ordinance forbidding chickens within seventy-five feet

100

of a dwelling, so we couldn't do the obvious thing, which was to put the goosehouse to its proper use. We had to build a new henhouse six feet farther away from the back door. This accomplished, we thought we had better get some expert advice on hens. We betook ourselves to the information office concerned with poultry. We got a good many answers to a good many questions, but the one that made us scratch our heads was a personal one. Robert always tries to be polite and is genuinely interested in human beings, so he asked the poultry expert how he had happened to get into educational work. "Well, I had a chicken farm upstate, but I couldn't make a go of it. I went broke and here I am." So much for experts!

It didn't take us long to find out how you can go broke on hens. We got a lovely setting of eggs and a broody Rhode Island Red. Here was our chance to inculcate sex education and the origins of life in the good healthy rural manner. The books that I had thrown in the garbage can had, after all, left some imprint. We set the hen, and after a time the eggs hatched. It was a fascinating performance to watch. I wouldn't have missed it for the world. Three dollars' worth of eggs, two dollars' worth of hen, five dollars' worth of grain, and we got twenty-four hours' worth of education. That night the rats took all the chicks.

We started again, this time with pullets. The experiment was more successful, that is, until the "pullets" started to crow and the Slaights called the police. The Slaights were within their rights. We were not allowed cockerels that crowed. The law forbids it. We sent for the poultry expert, who was asked to cull the roosters from the hens, and he showed us which to decapitate. We had fifteen dead chickens. Aunt Mary dressed them and I canned them in my beautiful canner. The next morning, just before dawn a shrill cock-a-doodle-doo pierced the sweet dreams of a low butcher's bill. Robert groaned, got out of bed, and with his hair on end staggered out to the "hen" house, where he snatched the still crowing culprit and wrung its neck. We eventually got down to real pullets.

I would quite often forget to grain them until late in the afternoon, but I always gave them a lot to eat and they laid profusely. Double yolkers were the order of the day. Once, however, I waited until sundown to feed those miserable hens. I opened the trough from the barn side and stood in a paralysis of nausea and desperate self-control while an army of rats poured out of the henhouse and down my slacks and across my feet. After that I never forgot to feed the hens in the morning.

We kept chickens, and we kept them successfully, but we learned the hard way. Chickens can get more diseases than any other creatures known to man. They also are stupid, lack any personality at all, and have horrible social aspirations. As soon as they are old enough to have an opinion, they become certain that they are the top kick of the barnyard. They peck each other and pull each other's feathers out until an order is established. One hen is immune to pecking from all the others; she pecks them. A second hen is pecked only by her, and she pecks all the others, and so on until the thirtieth hen, who pecks no one and is pecked by everybody. Anybody who wants to raise hens may. I loathe the silly things.

Anyhow we had eggs and chickens. We also had chicken manure and it is highly odoriferous. Aha, we would enlarge the garden and use the fertilizer! No waste of any kind must occur in a nation at war. Our chests swelled with patriotism.

We got a seed catalogue. There must be other things, new and different — things that we could grow.

Experience is presumed to be the best teacher. Before the year was over I had occasion to wonder what it is about gardeners that makes them immune to this type of indoctrination. Every year the seed catalogue arrives at our door, usually in the middle of the worst winter blizzard, when the thought of growing greens is sweet, and every year we sit by the fire thumbing through it, selecting and rejecting, but not much of the latter.

We list dwarf peas, and lima beans, remembering the never-to-be-equalled taste of last year's single panful. We determine that this year we will surely place the brush more carefully, sow in rotation, and reap meal after meal of mouth-watering legumes.

It never works out that way. It never has, and if history is any criterion to go by, it never will. Still, we think pridefully of the wonderful carrots that came from the garden on January 25 of one year and feel definitely superior to our fellow human beings who are forced to select parsley from the tired bunches at the market while we step down to the garden and get garnish and onions for our salads all year round. We continue to list packet after packet of vegetable seeds.

We know perfectly well that the birds will get a lot more of the strawberries than we shall, but we are forever trying new varieties of everbearings. We know that the borers will infest the squash, and that, at the time when ours ripen, the price in the market will be five cents a pound. We are fully aware of the fact that weeds grow apace, and that even chard grows slowly, but we persist in planting a garden.

It is uneconomical, it is hard work, it never comes up to expectations, but this year we shall surely be successful because we are driven by the greatest of all challenges — patriotism!

There are of course two schools of thought in the matter of garden lettuce — those who swear by it and those who swear at it. Lettuce, however, has one solid advantage — it always grows — and in chicken manure it grows superbly. Not quite as well as in goose fertilizer, but still! Say what you will, there are no tomatoes in the world that have the succulent flavor and the gorgeous color of those plucked full ripe from the vine.

Nor is there a woman with soul so dead that she does not thrill to the translucent crimson of homemade jelly. I handle a needle with the delicacy that I apply to a crowbar, but the Ladies' Aid comes around asking for my jelly for the church bazaar. And you should see the Duchess try to control her expression when *I* am asked how to accomplish such a culinary masterpiece!

Is there any smell on earth more delicious than that of freshly picked Concord grapes? I doubt it, for "the heady smell of wine" is a simile as old as the vine and as old as Noah.

It is a funny thing, though, how some people wince at the bragging words, "From our own garden." They always resent our implication that they should exclaim in wonder, but to us at Tongueslip, though we know it's impractical and that we would do better to visit the frozen food emporium, it seems that there *is* a difference in taste and in the quality of nourishment in vegetables from "our own garden."

Maybe our feeling goes back into unremembered time, when the planters of gardens gave man his first permanent home. Perhaps a man's roots go down with those of the seeds he plants, and take the same strength from a sense of belonging to the soil.

The seed catalogue "lies in its teeth" and we all know it. But it holds out a promise of things to come, so I say let it lie. Where else can I buy so much hope for so little money? After all, I always get lettuce and tomatoes, which is more than can be said for a lot of the utopias I've been promised in a lifetime of wars and rumors of wars.

[13]

IT'S no news that one thing leads to another, but the garden at Tongueslip has led to a lot. There used to be a lake where our cabbages grow; the shore line is still quite clearly marked by a terrace, and in aerial photos you can see the outline clearly.

The Watchung Indians used to camp by our lake, and General Washington's troops sat there quite often waiting for Christian Interest to mend their shoes. We turn up the evidence all the time: stone hatchets, skinning knives, arrowheads, bullets, buttons, and one afternoon Tommy found the lock of an old Kentucky long rifle with the flint still in it.

This of course made him very conscious of the treasures to be found under the earth, and he is now incapable of passing a pile of newly turned ground without making a careful examination of its contents.

That was how he found the shark's tooth. I still think somebody lost it, because it certainly does not belong in the Triassic shale of Central New Jersey, but find it he did, and show it to Aunt Mary he did, complete with dissertation upon paleozoology.

Aunt Mary belonged to the group referred to in the bosom of the family as "the frozen few," a phrase which came about through a gushing lady who approached our newly elected mayor and tried to persuade him that he should leave our church and join another. "Really, Your Honor, if you would just come along to us, you would meet the cream of the town."

"Yes indeed, Madam, the ice cream!"

Thereby "the frozen few" became a watchword, used by us to describe that incomprehensible group who are convinced that they, and they alone, are worthy of salvation.

Only the most admirable restraint prevents me from shoving them into the nearest mud puddle! They look at one so superciliously and, with solemn assurance, hold forth upon their possession of the one and only map of the one and only road which leads to the pearly gates. The uncompromising assurance with which Aunt Mary consigned the Unitarian minister to hell was one of the few thorns in the flesh I have ever been required to endure, but reviewing the fact that he was the only one in the poverty-stricken village of her origin who gave the children joy and recreation, taught them to read and to write, and introduced them to the Bible, I doubt very much if he *will* burn.

Salvation was a red-hot issue with Aunt Mary. It was absolutely contingent upon swallowing the Bible, jot, tittle, and comma, as the whale swallowed Jonah, in one unchewed gulp. It was fruitless to argue with her, and we seldom did. At ninety one is seldom amenable to suggestion. The light of the past shines in one's eyes to blind one, instead of over the shoulders to illuminate the path ahead.

Tom's fossil shark's tooth was bound to start a controversy. I should have known it, but I am related to the whale: I cannot keep my big mouth shut.

It seems to me that the magnificent story of the Creation as told in Genesis is in its essence gospel. One day, if you can, get an ancient rabbi to read it to you in the Hebrew. You will hear the silence at first, and then the thundering waves on some primeval shore, and the sonorous roll of that greatest of all poems will live with you for many a long year. It is only when you have heard it so read, and heard Beethoven's majestic music, " The Heavens Are Telling," that you *really* know and love that story, that you fully grasp the utter significance of the commandment, " Let there be light."

What a sight it must have been, that wild and storm-tossed sea, with no land to break the force of the wind around the whole circumference of the globe! With what wrenching and shuddering must the mountains have emerged from the deep, bare rock, jagged and colossal!

The seed of life from the lifeless void, at a Command, and the slow green growing on the rocky eminences, " For a thousand years in thy sight are but as yesterday! "

The creatures, behemoth, and the saurians thrashing through the primordial seas; the great forests, untenanted by birds, silent and soundless at first, and then teeming with song, and silenced again by the padding paws of the saber-toothed tiger.

The woolly mammoth crashing through the trees and grazing in great herds on the plains, while man, with only a mind to protect him, began to build his way of life and to reach upward with a sense of awe toward his Creator.

The great panorama of the universe spread like a canopy above him, the rich earth under his feet, the gift of fire, the knowledge of seedtime and harvest, the discovery of the wheel and the lever. What greater miracle has been wrought than this, and is a shark to be deplored because he shows this panorama to a child?

Aunt Mary thought so!

Tom's find was a beautiful specimen — shiny, perfect, a triangular fossil about four and a half inches high and some five inches across the base. The minute Tom saw it he knew what it was, because in the attic we had the jawbone of a nine-foot man-eater which Dad had caught in Florida. It was a horrendous maw, lined with row upon row of razor-sharp dentures, and it gaped threateningly even in death. Polly was scared stiff of it and I could scarcely blame her. It conjured up a harrowing image of horrific terror, thrashing in blue seas and pursued inexorably by a dark triangular fin.

A simple application of the formula for the area of a triangle, understandable to Polly and Mary K. because it involves only the base times the height, divided by two, gave us the size of the tooth. Then we measured the largest tooth in our known-length shark, took that area, and found out how much bigger the fossil shark must have been. We came up

107

with a length of one hundred and twenty feet, if the teeth of prehistoric sharks were in proportion to those of the present shark. It seemed reasonable to us.

Not so to Aunt Mary. She hit the ceiling! Her neatly braided white hair stood on end. Her sharp blue eyes spit fire. She held it as her dying creed that nothing had changed since the beginning of time.

When we asked her to explain the tooth, she dismissed it as a model, made by the Creator for reference purposes, and never endowed with life. Someone less pigheaded than I would have let the matter drop then and there. To me, at the time, it seemed of paramount importance to establish the existence of that shark. Probably it was a sort of psychological transference of egomania, but our son had a fish, a fish about which he would never have to lie, a fish one hundred and twenty feet long. What angler could resist!

I argued.

Aunt Mary showed me in no uncertain terms how wrong I was. Her bent shoulders straightened in defiance. In the first place the world was only five thousand years old. That could be proved by the measurements of the Pyramids, which were certainly larger and more important than this odd bit of rock Tom had found in the ditch. The world had not been in existence one hundred million years ago, and that was that. On the face of it our shark was a snare and a delusion!

The Duchess tried to silence me, but I would not be still. Was I to deny the evidence of all my senses, the laws of mathematics, and the facts of geological time for the whim of a nonagenarian? I was a scientist and *I* would show Aunt Mary how wrong she was!

It went on for hours. Histories were brought out, Darwin was quoted, slices of fossil-bearing rock were produced. Petrified wood was laid on the table. Ushabti figures from Egyptian tombs were declaimed upon. Aunt Mary sat in stony calm and pointed her gnarled finger to the first chapter of Genesis.

108

She did not get angry. Her voice never changed its pitch. Mine rose and spiraled until it had achieved the shrill of a tempest under the house corners. Aunt Mary was adamant.

"Dust thou art, and unto dust shalt thou return," she quoted. I thought I had her there. "What," I asked, "is going to happen then when the last trump sounds? Is there going to be a dust storm over the whole earth, a whirlwind, that will gather all the lost arms and legs and heads of soldiers from the far corners of the earth and deposit them neatly on the right people?"

"Order is heaven's first law; to God all things are possible." It was a flat and unanswerable statement. I was licked, and I knew it.

At that point Dad came in. "What's going on around here?" We both tried to answer him at once, but Aunt Mary won again. I was, she told my clerical father, bringing up his grandchildren as heretics, and she would *not* have it.

To my absolute amazement and complete fury, Dad swept my carefully arrayed evidence off the table. "Come on, Tommy. Let's put these back, then I'll show you how to use the slingshot like David. Only, remember, his wasn't rubber."

I was left to face Aunt Mary over the wide boards of the table. "Want a cuppa?" I offered peace tentatively. She nodded.

While the kettle boiled, I watched Dad and Tommy practicing with the lethal slingshot in the garden. Tom could scarcely draw the bands. Dad stood there with his pipe clenched in his teeth, grinning. I saw him take the sling and kneel, drawing the leather back to his cheek. He let go, and his precious pipe flew into a thousand fragments. He had forgotten that it stuck out into the trajectory of the stone!

Only yesterday I picked up one of the shattered pieces of that pipe. The melting snow revealed the mellow golden shard where the frost had worked it to the surface of the rosebed. I have started into shops a hundred times to buy another like it, before I remembered that Dad and Aunt Mary both know now the answer to the question, Who shall be saved?

I am still in ignorance and still wondering, very occasionally, but recently I read an article in an ultrascientific tome, an article that placed great emphasis on intellectual respectability. It gave me a jolt that brought the shark's tooth into focus as sharply as though it had all happened last week. For it seems that our earth came from star dust, and in some remote future, when the sun grows cold, it is, so modern science tells us, to that same dust that we shall return.

Aunt Mary never gave one single inch. She had her standards and she stuck to them. One of her standards concerned horses. I wish I had been old enough to know Dawson, her husband; he must have been quite a man. He was head groom on a large estate, and he trained the racers from the stable. Perhaps it was the very fact that Aunt Mary had long eaten the bread of a stable that convinced her of the inherent evil of the ponies. I don't know, but she hated them so that she would not even watch the Grand National Horse Show on the Loves' TV set.

I like horses and, in fact, earned my living, while getting my master's degree, by exercising and showing five gaited saddle horses and Tennessee walkers. Aunt Mary disapproved, and the one thing she would *not* polish was my riding cups, which stood in a row on the bookshelf.

The candlesticks from Gee Cross shone like gold, and she put the final patina on them with her bare hands. The silver for the table always gleamed. The andirons were immaculate, but my riding trophies could blacken to illegibility without her raising a hand, and I have always suspected that she enjoyed watching them do so.

I remember the quiet scorn with which she eyed me one day when I returned from a ride, muddy but unbowed. I had a palomino named " Cliquot," a very spirited horse, but, alas, she was what is known as " barn sour." If you could get her a hundred yards from her stall, all was well, but that hundred yards was a pitched battle. Her golden haunches tensed the minute I mounted, and her head, with its white mane, came back in a deliberate attempt to stun me as she reared. I was determined to teach her some manners, because it was a crying shame that such a beautiful creature should remain unmanageable. Cliquot and I had it out. I would mount and she would plunge. The point was to discover whether my temper or her stubbornness would first be lost. As a matter of fact, neither of us triumphed on that particular morning because the girth broke before either one of us had given way. I descended into a particularly deep mud puddle, saddle, bridle, and all.

When I walked in the door, Aunt Mary gave me one look and started to laugh. My blood, simmering already, boiled. I gave Aunt Mary a look that should have singed her eyebrows and stamped upstairs to the shower.

When I came down, Aunt Mary was polishing my riding cups in the kitchen. She turned her head over her shoulder and looked at me with her penetrating eyes.

"Thee canna stay on a horse, but thee can keep a civil tongue in thy head. Tha hast nae morals, but thy manners be excellent, that I'll admit. Here's a bit of polish for good manners at least."

I wanted to hug her. Ponies or no ponies, she was generous. But I didn't dare. If there was one thing Aunt Mary abominated more than horses, it was sentiment. For "tha canna be soft and last long in t'world."

She was of course a living proof of the fallibility of that statement. Still and all, between her stony determination to disapprove and my passionate affection for life and living, there must be some happy mean. Perhaps the children will find it.

You and I remember the fire horses, but to our children "horse" is just a term that expresses the power of an engine.

111

How I used to love to stand and watch at the firehouse! When the fire whistle blew, you really saw something!

At the Walnut Street firehouse they had three dappled grays. Their coats shone, and a Dalmatian lay at the door watching the men play checkers. Then, somewhere, a bell would set up an incessant clangor. The varnished shafts dropped beside the horses. Two men sprang to their sides and cinched the brass buckles. The dog jumped to its feet, ears pricked. The driver vaulted into his seat, and the hoofs clomped on the soft pine floor.

Down the street at a dead run, with the dog weaving between their feet, went the grays. Nostrils flaring, foam blowing from the bridles, sweat pouring from their shoulders, the fire horses went Sheol and leather! They made you want to cry, and they made you want to cheer: magnificent surging life, going to help someone who needed it, and they went all out.

Once, long, long ago, such a team pelted up Broadway. An ancient street cleaner was hosing the road in front of Trinity Church. He moved so deliberately that he seemed almost as much a fixture as the tombstones of Alexander Hamilton and Robert Fulton.

A little boy started across the street just as the galloping horses turned the corner. The driver saw the boy, but too late. He hauled back on the reins and skidded the fire horses to a stop on their haunches. The old street cleaner came suddenly to life, aimed his hose at the seat of the small boy's pants' and lifted him from under the pawing hoofs right into Trinity churchyard. This accomplished, he turned silently back to sluicing the roadway. Mr. Percy Morse, our good friend and neighbor, told me of seeing this episode just after the turn of the century. I wonder if the small boy himself is living and recalls it.

And the milkman's horse! How often its feet clopping through the dark before dawn have brought comfort to the ill in the knowledge that another night has passed! How often

112

as a child I heard that sound and knew, as though the town crier had called it, that "'tis four o'clock and all is well"!

We used to tie our sleds to the back of the milk sleigh in the afternoon and ride to the top of the hill, whence we could descend for two thrill-packed miles down the main street of town and onto the ice of the old canal. In summer we could jump onto the ice wagon and pick cold slivers from the chippings, to let them melt deliciously in our mouths. I like the slow pace of horses. It rests my weariness.

There were other horses too — the doctor's horse, the grocer's horse, and the somber blacks of what was then known as the "undertaker." (Was he so called because he put people under, or because he undertook a sorry task?) They would pass the church in slow procession with nodding black plumes and with checkreins tight. Somehow they lent to death a dignity and sense of eternity which in the hurry and bustle of motor hearses is lost in urgency and "Let's get on with it."

No, Aunt Mary, I still think that the great drays with eight teams in hand, turning on a dime, in perfect control, the gathered muscles of a hunter as it soars over a stone wall, the soft end of a horse's nose nuzzling the back of one's neck, and the sweetness of hay-laden breath are lovely things.

Surely if our Lord was born in a stable it need not be a place to scorn!

[14]

IT'S a far cry from fire horses to the mechanized warfare of our generation. However, we at Tongueslip were very much aware of the fact that we lived in the age of engines. Malcolm and Vin were both in the Air Force, and the inhabitants of our extra rooms were busy making propellers at Curtiss-

Wright. What really brought the engines of destruction into our own back yard was the Erie Railroad.

Tom, like all small boys, had trains on the brain. He ate, slept, and dreamed trains. He cut out pictures of trains. Eventually he himself became a train and could be seen chuffing and chugging up the driveway tracks, turning in the round-house barn, and eventually dragging a bright red caboose which other people, in their colossal stupidity, took for The Tra-Arn express wagon. Every day Tom, wearing his engineer's hat, Mary K., manning the caboose, and Polly, in the emergency car pram, were conducted to the switching yard downtown.

Tom knew, in 1943, the name of every major railroad in America. Since then a bridge has washed out up the line and there is no longer a direct connection with the tracks going west. If Tom were a little boy today, he would not be able to watch the freights roll by. In those days they did, locomotive after locomotive, car after car.

Gondolas from the Lehigh Valley, carrying coal and ore; tank cars from the Santa Fe laden with oil; flatcars from the Erie, with planes and tanks and guns; boxcars from the Canadian Pacific, loaded with grain — all the resources of a vast continent pouring in endless motion over the steel rails toward the ships in New York Harbor! The plugging laboring of the locomotives on the upgrade, the lonely call of a whistle at night, and a sense of wheels within wheels and strength growing to a titanic force, gave us hope.

There were other trains that made the heart heavy. They pulled in and out of the Penn station in Newark, and it was to one of these that we drove with Brother Vin.

We had not been in the station five minutes before I bitterly regretted Mother Arny's decision to come.

The place was jammed with boys in uniform: sailors with their white caps tipped jauntily over their eyes; pilots with their caps sagging from the weight of phones on many missions, their eyes sad and strained; raw recruits, swaggering in their new-found manhood; and tanned, weary men with the blue-piped caps of the infantry, snatching cat naps on the long wooden benches. They moved at a command across the marble-squared floor of the depot.

There were men with the sleeves of their uniform hanging empty, men hobbling on crutches with casts on their legs — or no leg at all; heads still swathed in bandages with eyes peering intently toward the gate where they expected to be met; rows of stretchers for the last lap of the trip to the Veterans' Hospital, and, far down the platform, under a single dim light which dissipated in the fog and smoke, wooden cases, flag-draped, silent, with an honor guard standing watch over them.

The MP's whistle sounded. The inane chatter with which we all try desperately to fill such a hiatus ceased, and arms went tight around slim bodies, young bodies, old bodies, pulling them close. Some lips said it aloud, but most left it hanging in the air, " Is this, then, for the last time? "

The train lurched forward, slowly at first, and the very young lovers could keep pace with the moving windows through which hands extended, held their own.

The wheels gathered speed, and one by one the clinging fingers slipped apart. We left in silence. Mother Arny's almost total blindness had, I felt, its advantages.

The next morning the papers screamed: " Trains collide in Lumberton, North Carolina! Hundreds injured, seventy-three killed, forty-seven servicemen die on way to duty."

Vin's train! Was he one of the forty-seven? Mother Arny must not wait, and wait, for news. I hid the paper, but instead of adopting the simple expedient of removing a tube from the radio, I took her downtown, where she surely would not hear it.

If Vin was a casualty, I wanted Robert around when the blow fell. We waited at the bus stop.

A young soldier was standing there, huddled against the wind, with his collar turned up to keep the sleet from stinging the back of his neck. His face was set and his feet, planted far apart, gave him an appearance of solidity which the smoothness of his cheeks denied.

Mother Arny stood next to him, and her hand strayed toward the cuff of the khaki coat. The boy, sensing her concern, spoke gently.

"What's the matter, Mother?"

She hesitated, custom striving with love, "I was wondering, Son, is the coat warm?"

His arm went around her shoulders. "Don't you worry about me, Grandma; I'm supposed to be taking care of you." He swung aboard the New York bus and was gone.

I left her in the dress shop and slipped across to the Western Union office. "If," I said, "a telegram comes for us about the troop train, deliver it at the parsonage, will you?" The man at the counter looked up, grasped the wheels of his invalid chair, and swung it across the room to the teletype. "There's nothing here. But I'll take care of it, Sister." He looked at me with the friendly concern of one human for another. "Quit worrying, will you? Chances are we'll never ring your doorbell. You look like you could do with some sleep, Sister. I'll let you in on something — no War Department telegrams are ever delivered after ten o'clock at night. So at nine fifty you can start to relax."

I walked back across the street in the kind of fog that in ordinary times would have been fatal. But gas-rationing saved my life, as it had the lives of ten thousand other people during that year. I stood watching Mother Arny across the shop.

A stranger had called her, "Mother;" she had called a stranger, "Son." The man at Western Union, who had always before been just a crisp voice on the other end of the phone, had called me, "Sister." Was it only in worry and fear and fright that we human beings could come together as a family?

116

Was war the only way to understanding; was anguish shared the only means to love? I wanted to reject that tragic commentary, to deny it, to affirm the beauties of peace and the advantages of prosperity. But somewhere, somehow, there was a confusion of words, words which I could not remember, that reminded me that the discovery of mutuality in sorrow was not new.

How hard I tried, how hard we all try, to outwit disaster. We plan, we weigh one thing against the other, and then we are reminded yet again that time and chance enter into all things.

My well-laid strategy backfired because of a recipe. Mother Arny wanted to make gingerbread and knew that I had a quart of milk that had gone sour. So it was that she was beside me when the doorbell rang. The Western Union " boy," a gaffer in his late seventies, handed me the dreaded yellow envelope. " They told me at the office you wanted it delivered here."

I took it and turned it over in my fingers. He stood there, shifting from one foot to the other. It finally dawned on me that he was waiting for a tip, and as I fumbled in the pocket of my jacket I thought irrelevantly, perhaps we haven't changed so much after all. I proffered the quarter and he shook his head, " No, ma'am, I was just waiting to pick you up if you fainted."

I didn't propose to faint, and I said so in no uncertain terms. Mother Kate took the envelope from my hands and tore it open. " Read it," she commanded.

" Missed first section, was on second. Kiss the wild goose for me. Vin."

The next thing I knew I was on the sofa, with the old man at my feet and Mother Arny at my head.

" Thank you very much, Child, but hereafter don't try to soften my blows for me." She marched into the kitchen, straight as a ramrod, and poured out a cupful of sour milk without spilling a drop. Such is the self-discipline of Mother Arny, who demands nothing of anyone else and everything of herself. It is a trait that seems bred in the bones of her forebears and of her children, and it presents those who do not know them with an insoluble personal equation.

Those who love the Arny family are used to their passion for sitting on hard chairs without touching the backs, and understand perfectly that they would deem it no hardship to subsist for the rest of their days on clear tea and dry toast. Yet when they provide for others they serve up every vegetable cooked in a half pint of heavy cream and dotted with butter. People connive to get Mother Arny's mashed potatoes cold, even out of the ice box!

How the family, and particularly Mother Arny, can combine the manners of Sir Walter Raleigh, the lean and hungry look of Cassius, and the disposition of Santa Claus, I am darned if I know!

Perhaps you can guess the mixed emotions with which I greeted the *fait accompli* that Robert's Aunty Fern was on her way east to join the convocation of the tribe.

I rather expected her to be a second edition of her mother, Great-grandmother Smith, whose neat small figure clad in black silk, and wearing four white ringlets down the back of her neck, was one of the storybook pictures of my childhood. My first personal encounter with Aunty Fern left me breathless. She was small and stooped, and her thick glasses made one feel that she saw everything and saw it magnified.

She was always dressed in conservative but contemporary clothes, and they always fitted her to perfection. Aunty Fern's slip never showed, physically, mentally, or morally.

Aunty Fern had the indelible marks of a woman trained and skilled in a profession demanding the most exacting accuracy. She had once been head nurse in Peter Bent Brigham Hospital at Boston, and the habit of command was still upon her. She had not been in the house twenty-four hours before I knew that I had met my match in stubborn determination.

Unfortunately her interests lay in precisely opposite directions from my own. I, for instance, was interested in getting the hens to lay. All food was expensive and good food was impossible to get. Aunty Fern was both cleanly and godly, but I think that in the bottom of her heart she put them in that order. I brought the eggs in from the henhouse and laid the basket on the kitchen table. They were spotless, but Aunty Fern's first official action at Tongueslip was to scrub them with Sapolio and a brush. My heart hit my heels. What possible neutral ground could be found?

Aunty Fern disapproved of me. There are few things more difficult to bear and more persistently obvious than the pressure of New England disapproval directly descended from the Plymouth Colony. I know its uncompromising weight, for it runs in my veins too, but there it is mercifully mixed with Irish humor, Indian stoicism, German thoroughness, French Huguenot fire, and Cromwellian rebellion.

I was terrified and walked with becoming softness through the intimate maze of personal relationships.

I read the *Christian Herald, The Congregationalist, Advance,* and *Council* from cover to cover, seeking safe ground for conversation. I sent my slacks to the dry cleaners. I washed the grimy fingerprints off the woodwork and scrubbed the front door. Aunty Fern was a lady; she never criticized. She never had to. Her silence was sufficient.

And then came April and the annual parade of children bearing cardboard boxes began. These boxes contain the waifs of nature rescued every spring when the children of men start their migration through the woods and fields after a winter of confinement. They grab everything which is not quick enough to escape them — fish, fowl, and reptile. I trembled inwardly. What would happen now? Birds in the parlor with broken wings; fledglings in the Pine Room, needing to be fed hourly; baby rabbits in the upstairs hall, where it is sunny; and a tiny squirrel in the kitchen close to the stove. Formula-warming in hot water to be fed to the furry; raisins being cooked for the fledglings; disorder everywhere.

And then suddenly order! Neat rows of dolls' nursing bottles scrubbed and cleaned. A tray with adhesive and sharp scissors for the mending of broken legs and shattered wings. At the moment when an obstreperous long-legged railbird kicked and squirmed, a pair of deft hands holding the fractured leg and applying the splint with a skill that I could never have matched. An incubator made for the rabbits, with an electric light bulb and an old photography thermometer to check the temperature. An oxygen tent for the cardinal with pneumonia, made from the Silex and a balloon. The longing to heal, the abomination of suffering, the instinct of mercy — Aunty Fern, R. N. in action!

I could not get the mashed eggs, dry flies, mockingbird food, and worms into the throats of the long-billed birds. Aunty Fern saw the possibilities of a cocktail muddler and a plastic straw. With the muddler for a plunger and the straw for a container, we shoved the food into the very crops of reluctant patients, and when pity demanded release from life for the hopelessly mauled, it was Aunty Fern who explained how care must be taken not to cause fright and struggle, and showed how this could best be done.

It was not only hungry birds, and the injured and orphaned victims of the Slaights' cats, who demanded her attention. Children at Tongueslip, like children everywhere, had measles, mumps, and chicken pox. It was Aunty Fern who read to them hours without end, who fixed their beds so that even the most wrigglesome convalescent presented a decent appearance to the doctor. It was Aunty Fern who saw in a flash the danger of Polly's illness and acted with speed and skill to save her in the few critical minutes before medical help could arrive, who rocked her to sleep, who tended her every need, and made of the frail tiny baby the huskiest of the lot.

120

No longer did I need to seek for common ground; it was there, all around us. Aunty Fern could listen, and Aunty Fern could understand. Disapproval swept out to sea like the ice from the river at the first spring thaw, and a summer warmth of devotion and affection grew between us.

Aunty Fern never compromised with cleanliness or godliness. Each week saw her room turned out and every bureau drawer in order. Each Sunday found her white-gloved in the proper pew. "Order is heaven's first law," was her watchword.

Time, the ancient enemy, marched on. Aunty Fern had invented a splint for birds which was a masterpiece. She took two toothpicks, wrapped them in cotton, and stuck them to adhesive. These she sandwiched with the sticky side in and the broken leg for a filling. The adhesive stuck to itself and to the leg, but Aunty Fern had done some careful research. She discovered that in fifteen days of exposure to weather, the tape loosened and fell off. Here was a means by which a bird could be treated and released which was a boon in the case of warblers, flycatchers, and other insect eaters, who if kept for the twelve days necessary for a fracture to set, died of starvation. If you tie a bandage to such a bird and release it, the loose ends tangle in the brush and the bird meets with disaster. The Fern splint simply pulls off, leaving three days' leeway for healing.

The birds prospered under her care but Aunty Fern herself grew perceptibly frailer. In time she could no longer bandage birds — her hands were too unsteady. Little by little her indomitable will to do for herself gave way before necessity, but it was a pleasure to serve her. Her appreciation was warm and genuine, and it put me to shame, for Aunty Fern did more for me than I could ever have done for her. She had ministered to my heart; I could serve only the wants of her frail body.

121

[15]

IN 1943, the Russians had encircled and captured the Nazi Army before Stalingrad, and a series of events had taken place in that bitter battle that were to have a marked effect on our whole future. We did not know that at the time; we knew only that we were weary beyond imagining of long hours, incessant teaching of first aid, endless overtime, ubiquitous boarders, and the constant concern for those we loved who were in the middle of the whole ungodly mess.

An invitation from Cousin Betty to visit at Cuttyhunk was welcomed with open arms.

Cuttyhunk would be peaceful! The sea was full of fish for the catching. Betty had lobster pots. There was an enormous garden full of fresh vegetables which we did not have to weed. There was a cow. We could undoubtedly pick up some of the offshore sea birds which we had never seen, and above all we adore the Frothinghams, and a visit with them would be heavenly.

There was, however, the problem of gasoline. Robert had always refused to register even for a B card, and Dad had never taken advantage of his extra clergy allowance. We did have two cars, Dad's and ours. I had five gallons of gas stored from a period of excessive energy when I had thought it a splendid idea to walk everywhere, and so we were able, with much calculating and siphoning, to start with a full tank, and several coupons to boot.

We had to drive to New Bedford, Massachusetts, and then take a small boat, called the *Alert*, from that port — roughly fifteen miles out to sea to the end of the chain known as the Elizabeth Islands.

We could not leave New Jersey before five in the afternoon. Some last-minute details at the factory had to be attended to, and that was that. We had planned to reach New Bedford by nine, and had made our reservations accordingly, but not without some consternation at the discovery that our rooms would set us back forty dollars for the night.

The last time we of Tongueslip had been in that lovely seaport town it had been a sunny, leisurely place, with white yachts tied to the wharves, old whaling men sitting on the steps smoking clay pipes, and grass growing between the cobblestones of the streets. Money, however, wasn't what it used to be and we were prepared for the worst.

We set out from the office, Robert, Dad, the Duchess, Tom, and I, with Mary K. in her crib in the back seat. Robert drove the worst part of the journey, across the meadows, through Jersey City and the Holland Tunnel, up the West Side Highway, and onto the abominable Boston Post Road.

The whole Atlantic seaboard was blacked out at that time. The top half of headlights had to be masked with dark paint, and the low beam cast only a dim glow on the road ahead. This, and consideration of our worn and irreplaceable tires, caused us to drive with care and caution.

We stopped at New Haven, and had a very inferior supper, and Tommy was incessant in his demand for gum. I loathe gum. It gets into everything and, what is worse, it degrades the human countenance into a caricature of a ruminant, but for the sake of sweet peace I bought several packages.

Tommy promptly jumped for joy, slipped, and cut his chin wide open on the corner of the table. By the time that had been attended to it was eight o'clock, and we still had a hundred and fifty-five miles to go. That does not sound far, but if you ever drove with those accursed black-out lights you will understand that it seemed a hundred and fifty thousand.

Through Middletown, Portland, Cobalt, and Marlboro, Robert drove with consummate skill and safety. He has some extrasensory perception which enables him to follow a completely invisible road in dark or daylight. In daylight it is apt

123

to be so invisible that it ends up in a squirrel track going up a tree, but that is neither here nor there.

This time we did not get lost. We plugged manfully on to Willimantic, where it became my turn to drive again.

Bob got into the back seat with the children. Tommy had by that time asked every question but, "How far is it?" He latched onto that one and repeated it *ad nauseam*, every tenth of a mile. I gave him some gum to keep him quiet.

The temperature dropped and fog rolled in from the coast. It boiled in damp billows into our faces and condensed on the windshield. The headlights made no dent in it. I crawled the interminable miles. Up and down, rise after rise, with the black top blending into the fields and the pastures, we crawled through the night. There was no traffic, but one inexorable shadow, too lazy to pick his own way, hung hour after hour on our taillights.

I peered intently through the darkness ahead, and saw a sodden man walking on the shoulder of the highway. The mist swirled in spectral shapes, and suddenly the pale fourth horse of the Apocalypse reared up before me. Nostrils flaring, hoofs pawing the air, he came straight at us in a dead run down the road. Time slowed to an interminable drag. If I turned out to the right, I would kill the man on the shoulder. If I turned to the left, the horse would go straight through the window onto our children. If I hit him head on, he would come through the windshield onto my parents and myself.

It was one of those nightmare choices which most of us have examined academically in the middle of a sleepless night and shaken off when the cold sweat soaked the sheets.

Life is sweet for me. I had not the slightest desire to die a heroic death. The jungle screamed in my ears, "Let go of the wheel and duck," but I saw the Duchess beside me looking at Dad with a "This is it" look in her eyes, and I saw him lean so that he was between her and the windshield.

There was a choice! If I could turn at an angle, just the

124

right angle, I could clip the off shoulder of the horse and he would ricochet off. I was not behind the eight ball; I could use my knowledge of billiards. My guardian angel must have snatched the wheel — I slammed my feet down on the brakes and steered for the crucial spot.

Billiards paid off. The screaming, neighing monster catapulted over the hood, hit the road, and disappeared into the darkness. A rending crash sounded at the back of the car, and my head was slammed down on the steering wheel as though it had been tapped with a pile driver. The children were instantly and violently sick.

We got out to inspect the damage and I found that my knees had a strange tendency to turn inward and my tummy a violent urge to turn over.

The driver of the car that had crashed into our rear started to curse all women drivers, saw Robert's lips tighten, and refrained from further comment. He had plowed into the back of us like a bulldozer, and of course he had no insurance. What was a good deal more serious was that the precious gasoline was dripping steadily from our tank.

Tommy, with the hardy thrift of childhood, had rescued his gum. I snatched it and stuffed it into the hole in the gas tank.

At that moment a state trooper on a motorcycle pulled up and started asking questions. When I told him what had happened, he looked at me pityingly and sniffed my breath obviously. "Where," he demanded, "is the horse?"

We scoured the countryside for the horse and never saw so much as a hair of his mane. I was called to order by the officer in no uncertain terms. Robert waited until that gentleman was all through and then beckoned to him and pointed to the ventilator. There, not six inches from the windshield, was a bloody horseshoe complete with nails. I will say for the trooper that he apologized handsomely and turned his attention to the culprit who had been sitting on my tail all evening. A tape recording of that would indeed be a collector's item, but the trooper wouldn't even give me the horseshoe.

Finally we were told to go ahead on our way, and we limped into New Bedford at 3 A.M., still slowly dripping gasoline, and bucking at very bump. We entered our forty-dollar rooms, undressed the children, and fell into bed. The *Alert* sailed at crack of dawn. Even at twenty dollars an hour those beds were worth it! Money isn't what it used to be.

Routed out by the room clerk's call, we went down to breakfast. The smell of bacon, almost forgotten, assailed my nostrils — coffee, black and strong, gave an aroma to the day. We ate heartily and went down to the wharf.

Robert made arrangements to have the car repaired while we were on the island. Two young shore patrolmen looked over our various and sundry credentials. They made us empty our wallets and show every card we had. Dad's birdbanding license was in his cardcase. They turned sharply as a man took out a camera to snap their picture, and converged on him. They impounded his camera, they impounded his binoculars. I was surprised that they did not impound his pants when I heard what he called them. They were polite but definite.

" This is a military zone; we can't take any chances."

I stood quite still, determined not to let my eyes wander in the direction of *my* binoculars, which were in plain sight in Mary K.'s bassinet.

The youngest man went over to Dad. " You're a birdbander — Fish and Wildlife Service? "

" Yes, officer."

" Well, if you're a birdbander you should know what I learned my first year at it. Young birds chill easy. Put another blanket on that baby. Also, there's dovekies on the island."

We boarded the *Alert* and set out to sea. Every sea bird in Pough or Peterson went over. We endured the loss of many species for our life list!

Dad's cardcase and Robert's " go anywhere " identification had satisfied the shore patrol, and we still had our glasses

126

and cameras under Mary K.'s blanket, but it seemed hardly kind to rub it in.

We soon discovered the reason for the screening. A plane screamed overhead and dropped a bomb on a small rock in the middle of nowhere. Water spouted from the near miss and a deafening explosion roared across the water. On the horizon a target drawn by a cutter moved in zigzags, and the shore battery let them have it.

Even if you know it's not you they're aiming at, there is a certain very unpleasant sensation in having artillery flung over your head! We knew now why the edict of "no glasses"! The flashing guns could very easily be located from our vantage point. I found myself praying that the boys in those emplacements were good at mathematics.

In a few days we got so we didn't flinch at every bomb. In fact, we watched the runs with fascination and soon were able to recognize the pilots from the way they came out of the sun and down onto the target.

We didn't do much birding. Dad and Robert felt that we should not use the binoculars except on the far shore of the island. I guess their premise was a good one: "What you don't know you can't inadvertently tell." Perhaps they remembered the top brass that discussed the routing of radar tubes at our house one night in a roomful of people they'd never met before. A route-change order was on the wires before the brigadiers' taillights got out of the driveway — which was a lot of unnecessary work for a lot of weary people and is one reason I made it my business not to know anything ever.

I was sorry not to see the dovekies. I still have never seen one, but the blessed sensation of not having to watch one's tongue is worth it.

I live in deadly terror of the day when under anesthesia, or in complete fury, I shall babble the loves, hates, parentage, and previous condition of servitude, of all the people who,

127

mistaking me for a father confessor, have poured the story of their lifetime into my unwilling ears. Surely it is asking a lot to expect someone else to keep secret what you yourself cannot hold inviolate!

There are things besides birds on Cuttyhunk, however, and, like most things that we enjoy, they are not curtailable by edict or by directive. The fields and roadsides of the island are heavy with the scent of new-mown hay, and the bramble thickets hold a rich harvest of blackberries for the picking.

What is better, more soul-satisfying, than the smell, sight, and taste of a deep-dish blackberry pie? Particularly when one has had the foretaste of blue-stained fingers, a few odd scratches here and there, the competition of rose-breasted grosbeaks, catbirds, and thrushes for the berries.

I remembered a scene long forgotten of an August day when the countryside was full of tattered small fry picking berries into lard pails. We too were berrying, but not peddling our wares to the cityfolk. Perhaps we were not even then enterprising enough, but I recalled the scathing glance of one small boy who looked at me up and down and remarked: "You must be crazy, coming here with a Pierce Arrow and a chauffeur to pick berries. You could buy them easier."

Probably because I was very small, and unable to comprehend the economic problems involved in the remark, I did not defend myself with the explanation that neither of the outward marks of what it pleases the ignorant to call "success" belonged to us. If I had tried to do so, it would still have been impossible to explain all the reasons why anybody who didn't have to go berrying would want to. Even then there must have been something that impelled me toward the fields.

Perhaps it was the flashing feathers of the bluebirds, the penetrating odor of mint and thyme and pennyroyal, the hot sun on the back of my neck, or the cool sound of the rippling brook which ran beside the briers.

There was still, at Cuttyhunk, something challenging about berrying. The largest, ripest, most luscious berries are always in the heart of the bushes. Those on the outside tend toward a scrawny dryness.

There is always a bush, heavy-laden, just across the swale, which demands the gamble, usually lost, that one will successfully elude both mud and water and a spilled pail, if one jumps with sufficient accuracy.

There is the necessity for restraint in refusing to eat the tempting fruits until the pail itself will hold no more, and there is in all these things a sense of the rightness of doing them, for the reward is immediate, certain, and predictable.

Those who fear scratches, those who will not blacken their hands, those who dare not wet their feet, will never taste the true deliciousness of life or of deep-dish blackberry pie.

⌐16⌐

TOM'S grim picture of shore police had dimmed at Cuttyhunk and now his dream of the FBI men was due for a rude awakening. Conditioned by Dick Tracy, he was sure that all G men wear trench coats, pull their hats well down over their eyes, and keep their right hand in their pocket to assure a speedy draw.

The G men who called at Tongueslip were the counterparts of Mr. Peepers. They asked the weirdest questions about the parish! For instance, why should Mr. Hoover care if Jeff ever helped his father by mowing the lawn, and what earthly connection is there between an interest in postage stamps and the Manhattan project?

The whole situation had an aura of complete unreality.

From being begged to maintain silence and discretion, we were ordered to spill the entire contents of the mental bean pot.

On one occasion a diffident young man rattled the silver sleigh bells and, upon being admitted, gulped out the fact that he was investigating F. V. Arny. Did Dad know him?

With a twinkle, Dad allowed as he did.

F. V. Arny was presently in the Air Force as a meteorologist. Was he inclined to gossip?

The answer was a categorical "no" — but I couldn't help wondering what difference it could possibly make if Brother Vin should talk about the weather.

Perhaps after all these years his great-great-grandfather, the clam, was about to be vindicated. His dominant chromosomes have descended from generation unto generation, and that's for sure. The family *never* speak about anything which could, by the wildest stretch of the imagination be construed as personal, confidential, or even moderately club chatty. They have one relative who has been known to comment that he thought there might be a frost on Monday, but they think he talks too much.

The odd thing about it is that they know more about the ancestry, connections, private lives, opinions, political ramifications, and general health of the community than anybody else in it. Maybe that's why! One supposes, if one examines the human physiognomy, that since we have two ears and one mouth, we are supposed to listen twice as much as we talk, but it's hard on a hostess if *everybody* does that.

Anyhow, Mr. FBI Peepers seemed perfectly satisfied about Brother Vin, and during the next few years he became a constant caller at Tongueslip.

On one occasion he cornered me about a neighbor who was being considered for a very hush-hush job in Russia.

"Do you know him well?"

"Very."

" Is he honest? "

" Yes."

" Is he discreet? "

" Yes."

" Mrs. Arny, I sense a hesitancy. What's the matter? "

" Nothing."

" I think there is."

" O.K. I'll tell *you*. He's married to a darling girl, he has three lovely children, and to my certain knowledge he is running around with a chippy who is making a fool of him."

" So."

" So I think a man who would cheat on his wife could conceivably cheat on his country — maybe not, I don't know."

The FBI man put his wallet back in his pocket and got up. " Well, I do."

He was not Mr. Peepers at all. In that split second he was himself, and I understand completely the success of the FBI.

If some brash young salesman had appeared at our door and asked questions, he would never have arrived at first base. " Mr. Peepers," by his very manner, assured me that he hated butting in, and knew we hated helping him to, and convinced us that if *he,* the epitome of meekness, felt called upon to act, surely we could do no less than co-operate. Mr. FBI Peepers could have made a fortune on Broadway. He preferred the anonymity of serving his country.

We were glad that most of what we had to say to him was pleasant. There is something terribly satisfactory in being able to say unequivocally, " Ed, Jane, Carol, Jack — straight as a die, uncorruptible."

When you balance your judgment of an individual against the safety of your country, you are careful. It is good to realize how utterly you can trust most of your friends and neighbors.

There were some who hoarded sugar, some who patronized the black market regularly, but the vast majority of them took the bitter with the better and did what they could.

131

There wasn't really much we could do except save fat and not waste paper, and collect scrap metal. I was very glad of the metal drive. We had three old boilers in the cellar which no one would take away for love or money, and then all of a sudden they put our block on top of the list for weight of scrap collected. Two defunct lawn mowers, several old stoves, and yards of copper leader with holes in it were also removed from the premises. I wonder if that's where the wrought-iron thistles went? If so, it was in a good cause.

Suddenly the war impinged with a direct personal impact rather than unified group concern. The New Jersey divisions had entered the combat zone. Where the names on the casualty list had been of remote though grave concern, they became familiar and conjured up visions of happy little boys with baseball bats playing in the side yard.

It was impossible, incredible, unspeakably horrible, that they were lying sprawled in the mud of the jungles, or on the deserts of Africa, or falling in flames toward the castles on the Rhine.

The only son of one of my dearest friends was reported missing over Germany. His mother walked very straight and very carefully. Her control and courage were magnificent but brittle, and her hand kept straying to the wings which she wore always above her heart. Others of our friends were certain of their loss. Some bent under the blow, others broke.

The waves of the North Atlantic swept the decks of the escort ships and left a glare of ice behind. A sudden lurch, and young Howland was listed as "lost at sea."

Closer and closer the long lists rolled. Gold stars showed with agonizing clearness on the bronze plaque in the church. There was nothing we could do but pray.

I don't know to this day how they stood it, any of them, waiting, watching, hoping. Of course it was worse abroad. Letters from our family in England made that abundantly clear. We were able to get some parcels to them by one means or another, but what we sent was pitifully inadequate.

The cold, wild Atlantic rolled between us, and its waves washed relentlessly on the white shore where we went when we could to watch for the sea birds and to escape the interminable telephone and the incessant radio.

Sometimes we would sight a convoy of tankers coming up the coast with their cargo of lifeblood for the war of machines. Sometimes the sand was not white but black, streaked with the oil which the U-boats had spilled, and the sodden water fowl, tarry and helpless, brought the plight of the men into horrible focus.

Once, just outside the breakers, we saw what we first took to be a cluster of ducks, but as it turned over and over in the surf we recognized it for what it was, and phoned in to the Coast Guard lest some brave man lie in sprawled disfigurement, a cynosure of morbid eyes and gaping mouths invading even the privacy of death, upon the shore he gave his life to save. This last indignity he could be spared and was.

We could do nothing for the men, and very little more for the birds, but we did manage to save Ezekiel.

Ezekiel is probably the only old squaw duck who ever attended a deacons' meeting. When Nubs Vernon picked him up it was impossible to determine whether he was a bird or some new variety of mine. He moved — and that was all.

The board of deacons met that night at Tongueslip and they evinced a surprising amount of interest in Zeke. One of them suggested that we wipe whatever it was that we had with Crisco. This we did. Kerosene was fine for removing the oil from clothes, but it would have burned Zeke's skin horribly. We Criscoed him and wiped him and washed him in Lux and warm water. Eventually he emerged from the tub recognizable as an old squaw duck. We dried him and he preened himself — and next morning we took him to the lake to release him.

Old squaws are sea ducks, but we figured he'd have to fly

the ten miles to the ocean himself. We dared not waste gas on that.

We set him in the lake and he promptly sank. All we could see of Zeke was his head, sticking up like a periscope. Not only the tanker oil, but the oil that protected his feathers from wetting had come off with the soap. Ezekiel was on shore leave till spring molt.

We fed him canned mussels and goldfish, but he didn't like them much, and not wishing to have him starve to death, we sent him to the zoo.

There we learned that the war was affecting other animals too. The flamingos were snow-white. The shrimp which they used to eat were brought in by ships and so were no longer obtainable. The substitutes lacked some unknown factor and the flaming plumage faded as a result.

Not that one dreams for a moment that a comparison could or should be made between birds and men, but simply as a matter of record, hundreds of thousands of dovekies, ducks, plover, and phalaropes were casualties of the war. Not from the guns, but from the oil slicks spread by the U-boats and by the sinking ships which took so much of the nation's heart to the bottom of the seven seas.

The world was on fire — and all we could do about it was buy bonds, flatten tin cans, and talk about it.

Father Arny thought about it.

He sat in his chair by the window and, though his body was helpless, his mind stretched forward into the future and shuddered at what it saw.

He was a scientist; he was aware of the sea as the rest of us have never been aware of it. He saw it as a vast reservoir of energy, waiting, waiting, for men to unravel its secret, and I remember the day when he sat with Mary K. asleep on his lap and looked down at her with sadness.

"Someday, Child, a man will find the secret. He will tear the waters of the ocean apart, and he will make of it an ex-

134

plosive weapon of whose power there is no end. I pray that I shall never see that day."

I took Mary K. still sleeping and put her in her crib.

That night his prayer was answered. Two messages flashed to the Air Force bases and Vin and Malcolm started the journey home.

We watched and we waited, and fitfully we slept, and then in the night the heavy tread of boots came up the stairs.

" We caught a ride in a B-29 from the coast. Are we in time? "

The answer was yes — just in time. Father Arny knew them. But war cannot wait on the death of the old. It is incessant in its demand for the young. As quickly as they had come, Vin and Malcolm were gone again and the house was lonelier than ever.

Every hour, on the hour, over WMCA *The New York Times* brought us important news bulletins and I got as far away from it as I could.

June 6, 1944, was a beautiful day. The sun shone on the perennial borders in the garden at Tongueslip, and the scarlet poppies nodded in a gentle breeze. The most pressing business I had to attend to was the worship service for the executive board of the Ladies' Aid.

Suddenly the church bell began to toll. I thought nothing of it. Quite often someone grabs the bell rope instead of the dumbwaiter rope — but the ringing continued in slow, surging rolls and I went to see what had happened.

The church doors were flung wide and the candles on the altar were lighted. People were streaming toward the door from the nearby stores.

The rubbish truck clanged down the street and drew up at the curb. Two men jumped from the running board and stalked warily into the sanctuary, hats in hand.

Someone spoke quietly to " Do " Hupfeld and he walked into the organ loft. The soft humming of the bellows could

135

be heard in the utter stillness, and then the organ pealed forth in stately measure.

> " Eternal Father, strong to save,
> Whose arm doth bind the restless wave,
> Who bidd'st the mighty ocean deep
> Its own appointed limits keep:
> O hear us when we cry to Thee
> For those in peril on the sea."

Dirty from gardening as I was, covered with flour like the baker, in a bloody apron like the butcher, smeared with oil like the grease monkey from the garage, carrying babies and groceries like the housewives, in shirt sleeves like the tavern keeper — they came and they prayed for the lives of their sons and for the liberation of a continent on D-Day.

Perhaps that is why they were heard. Perhaps that is how we should go to God — with the evidence of our labor upon us and the dignity of our calling manifest.

[17]

THE British took Bayeux on June 7, 1944. Carentan fell on June 13. The United States took Cherbourg on June 27. The British and Canadians took Caen on July 9. The Third Army attacked St. Lo, and the Canadians took Falaise. The Argentan Gap was sealed, and on August 25 the French and the Americans entered Paris.

And the price?

Well, we were used to high prices, and victory was in sight. Arthur's mother didn't feel that way, nor Bill's. What must the bitterness of anguish be to lose one's son with safety quite in sight? The hand grasping the flung life line and slipping, the feet touching the narrow ledge and missing, the pulse surging and stopping!

At Ardennes, General von Modell made a desperate counter-attack. The Third Army scattered toward the Bulge, while at Malmedy the Nazis cut down the captives with machine guns and left them screaming and dying on the field. "American losses estimated at forty thousand."

More stars on the bronze plaques, more families bending and breaking in the storm.

They were not the only ones who broke. Young scientists trained from childhood to love and serve their fellow men beat out their brains seeking to justify the application of their knowledge.

I used to go canoeing years ago with a young man who dreamed of making a lens that would span the universe. He helped to make one to destroy cities. The last time I saw him he was sitting in the reception room of an asylum, staring into the wide space he had hoped to conquer and picking erratically at shreds from oakum. I wiped the spittle from his chin — I have never gone back.

Iwo Jima was invaded by the United States joint expeditionary force on February 19, 1945.

Crawling on their bellies, with their fingernails worn to the quick in the volcanic sand, the forces of the United States of America took Iwo Jima, and three Marines, one an American Indian, set up a flag on Mount Suribachi.

Okinawa — United States casualties, forty-nine thousand one hundred and fifty-one. Whose son was the one?

May 7, 1945. Unconditional surrender signed by the Germans at Reims, and the cathedral windows could now be safely replaced. But what of the cathedrals, and the straw huts, and the bamboo and paper houses in the Pacific?

I tried to push them out of my mind and could not. So much that is beautiful at Tongueslip was made by the skillful hands that built those buildings: the silk screen on the piano, the

137

Satsuma cups, the rice-pattern bowls, the willow plates. The very garden blooms with the scarlet hinodejiras in spring and in fall with chrysanthemums. The dwarf cypress in the rockery, the retinisporas in the border — all are the product of a nation that worships beauty. How — how — have we ever gotten into such a tangled, twisted, tortured mess with our fellow men?

The radio blared: "On to victory — tighten your belts for the last lap — buy Bazoola's extract for your liver, and spell it backward."

How I loathed that commercial! The transition from laxatives to mortal sorrow and back jarred my molars. Was the whole world more concerned with its own bowels than with millions of men who were going through hell? Sometimes I know that I was selfish too and I hated myself.

I did not allow my anger to extend to the older generation. It is nigh onto impossible to change the habits and outlook of people between seventy and a hundred. The family at Tongueslip had four in this category. For half a century they had had butter on the royal slice of bread, porterhouse steak on Wednesday, and prime ribs of beef with Yorkshire pudding for Sunday dinner.

Polly and Mary Katharine had ration books, and I get a chuckle out of the careful descriptions: Age, three days; eyes, blue! Dear Pauline! Who else would have come to visit a new baby and its mother, ration book in hand? Only Pauline who, as my maid of honor, had presented me with a driver's license properly made out to Mary Arny, just as we stepped into the car amid a shower of rice!

There is a connection, you see, between the very old and the very young. Since Polly was still eating on my rations, and Mary K. was on a bottle, I had for a while enough red coupons to retain the Sunday roast, and enough sugar to avoid the necessity of curtailing Dad, who always poured four spoonfuls into everything and *never* stirred it. Butter was my problem.

For a while I considered the purchase of a cow, but the Slaights were already bitterly complaining of my hens, and I was terribly tired of wringing the necks of cockerels the minute they crowed! Who could muzzle the mooing of Bossy? Pigs would have been all right — there is no ordinance against *them* in Montclair — but pigs don't give milk.

I refused to bow to the black market even to retain the family equanimity. It was not that my octogenarians meant to be difficult — it was just that they were so polite about it all that I could have murdered them. I hit upon a scheme, a veritable stroke of genius. I would get the Duchess to do the marketing!

She acquiesced immediately. The version of what happened is from — you guessed it — the Ladies' Aid, now the Women's Guild.

Cape flying, cane clicking, the Duchess marched into Mr. Holly's excellent butcher shop. A chair was found for her immediately and she was enthroned. Mr. Holly asked her wants. " Five pounds of stew meat, please."

He brought it out and laid it on the block. She gave the grizzly war-time fat one scathing look. " I think something better than that, please! "

He retired to the freezer and brought out a T-bone steak. She prodded it, asked to have it turned over — bought it — and marched out. Everyone was so surprised that coupons were never mentioned.

I was not surprised, having heard the story, to receive a bill for meat that practically ruined my budget for the month. After that I did my own shopping. Mr. Holly helped me.

Meanwhile coffee was rationed, and shoes. I made a horse deal with the elderly. The children's coffee ration and mine, for four shoe coupons. Tommy and Mary K. went through at the sole in two weeks and the uppers in a month.

Still, presence never is denied. The Duchess had an engagement in New York. I took her. We were to meet Mrs. DeGolyer at the Waldorf. We managed to get a cab, after considerable waiting, and the disgruntled driver made the common indifference of wartime cabbies very plain. I put Mother in the cab and gave the address.

When we arrived there was, of course, no doorman. The Duchess sat erect and calm. She was on the door side; I was helpless.

The cabby turned and glowered, "Watcher waiting for?"

Her voice was completely serene: "For you to get out and open the door for me."

He did!

How could I say, "There is no butter," to people like that? I bought cream and churned it.

Yet this is the anomaly of Tongueslip's ancients. They gave blood by the quart, calmly stating their age as "over twenty-one" and daring with a glare the Red Cross aides to question them further. They never complained that the house was cold when the oil ration gave out, but put on extra sweaters, and behaved as though everything was perfectly normal.

When the pipes froze, they carried slops with never an upturned nose. They cleaned chickens, canned food, made preserves, but butter they had always had and butter they proposed to eat. You figure them out — I never could! I only wish that I could really portray them as they are.

Probably everybody has at one time or another wished he could paint. I never see the Duchess, seated in her wing chair in the Pine Room, hands crossed on the top of her cane, straight features and high cheekbones clear-cut by the light of the hearth fire, that my fingers do not itch for a brush.

The same tableau presented itself each day, and each day she listened calmly while the radio shouted, "Every hour on the hour, over WMCA *The New York Times* brings you important news bulletins." That phrase is engraved on my mind with such clarity that I am sure I shall babble it on my deathbed.

Dad got up and went to the map, prepared to move the little pins once more. I hated those little pins! Black for the German Army rushing across Europe; red for the United Kingdom moving inch by inch back toward the square green markers for the fleet. As I watched them they turned into little figures, wrestling and struggling against a hand that moved them willy-nilly across the vast panorama of Mercator's projection.

I could never look at it coldly, as a matter of logistics. I always thought of the pathetic streams of men, women, and children, swept before the onrushing tide of pins; shattered, shoved, ignored, in a battle that they neither wanted nor understood. But I was held, in spite of myself, by a fascination in the horrifying game, much as I suppose the more civilized Romans stared at the revolting spectacles in the Circus Maximus.

Even now when the pins were moving the other way, little yellow pins retreating back from the islands of the Pacific, blue pins surging across the Dark Continent, the black line in France and the Benelux countries wavering, breaking, dissolving — even in the midst of victory — it was people, carrying their pitiful possessions, dying in ditches, crying in hunger, that haunted me.

I can understand the glory of a battle such as that between David and Goliath. I can feel a surge of grandeur at the twanging of long bows and the clanking of armor, and the rushing of chariots. Here skill counted, and personal courage. Where is the glory of a blockbuster?

Perhaps that is why we all turned to chess at Tongueslip.

Professor and ditchdigger take to it with equal enthusiasm. In moving the men across the checkered squares, kings and knights, queens and pawns march at the command of each protagonist in matched armies. Here on this little inlaid table a battle of minds rages. No factory, however great, bears influence. No ancestor, however blue his blood, intrigues within

141

the court and builds disaster in exchange for gold. There is no Quisling and there is no propagandic lie. Skill and skill alone can conquer.

And what a revealing game it is! I dare say a man's chess betrays him quicker than his hands. Some move in intricate patterns, seeking to surprise. Others keep closed ranks where no risk loses hope of gain. Some play close watch on every square. Others cast pawns to the edge with ruthless unconcern. Some clear the decks and fight it out with king and queen alone.

The Duchess took all comers, and in the end emerged the champion. One looked at her game and thought one saw the checkmate three moves off, and then from somewhere, as a stallion guided by a rider who has joined forces with it, a knight would gallop to the crucial square, backed by a bishop, and the game was done.

Her old hands, long and slender, graced by a single ring, so simple as to become magnificent, would fall to her lap in the perfection of repose, and the next opponent would pull up a chair and draw the battle lines.

Dad could never bear to be beaten. He would play and play. With each defeat his jaw would set more firmly, and he would move with greater care. Sometimes he would sit until midnight, making each move with lightning speed until the very vitality of his aggressiveness would wear his opponent into a somnambulistic slip.

My own chess game is erratic. I hate to beat anyone except the Duchess. If they are discouraged, I always want them to win, yet hesitate to throw the game lest they discover it. If they are angry, it is much better that they should win and get it out of their system. But when they are cool and calm and sure like Mother, something arises in me that make me play like a fiend, and I sometimes beat her because my attack is never orthodox.

It was in the middle of such a game that the news of Hiroshima flashed over the radio. We did not really hear it the first time. So much had been said, over and over, for so long, that we listened with our ears and not our minds. But as I moved a castle to the queen's knight's fourth, the voice finally penetrated my concentration on the game.

Squares? Squares? $E = MC^2$?

I felt a sudden violent nausea as must everyone who has ever labored in a laboratory with facts, figures, apparatus, and devotion, seeking to make a slightly better world. Energy equals mass times the square of the speed of light!

"They have undone us!"

The pity of it, the waste, the fruitless, anguished birth of knowledge without wisdom.

August 6, 1945. Hiroshima, Japan, population three hundred and forty-three thousand nine hundred and sixty-nine. Dead, seventy-eight thousand one hundred and fifty. Injured, thirty-seven thousand four hundred and twenty-five. Missing — no trace — thirteen thousand eighty-three!

Entry in pilot's log — two words — "My God!"

We, the little people, called on our Maker. They, the pilot and crew, mentioned Him officially. Where are the kings, the princes, the potentates, and the diplomats who sat in their offices and palaces moving us like pawns across the chessboard of destiny? Do they call upon heaven? Or is it no accident that the end of a game that began in the Pacific two thousand years ago is "*sheik mati*" — "checkmate" — the king is dead?

[18]

VICTORY was in sight! We decided to celebrate with a picnic. I packed a lunch while Robert and Tommy went out to the compost heap to dig worms for bait.

Off we set for Indian Lake on roads filled with cars. Gasoline was no longer a matter of life and death. Soon there would be plenty. To the victors belong the spoils!

We parked on a little bypath and walked in to the water's edge. We were alone except for a white egret wading mechanically in the shallows, and the swallows dipping for water on the glassy surface of the pond.

Robert baited Tom's hook and he threw in. The red and white bobber danced in the sun. The small boy watched it with intent concentration. Mary Katharine dug in the sand by the shore with a wooden spade and watched the water come up in every well. Polly, clad only in a red bandanna, kicked in the sun, discovering those marvelous items, her toes.

Robert leaned against the bole of a pine tree, contentedly puffing on his pipe. For the first time in years his shoulder showed no sign of twitching.

Slowly the knots inside me loosened in the sun. I had not realized how tight they were — nor how many. I watched an eagle circle in the cloudless heavens and wondered idly if it was an omen. Surely it was very early; perhaps it had a nest in the vicinity, though that was hardly likely.

A wild yell interrupted my lazy thoughts and a wet and wiggling sunfish catapulted out of the water and into my lap. I removed it from the hook and held it up for our young angler to admire.

Mary Katharine looked at it: "Oh! a technicolor fish. Put it back quick, Tommy. It can't breathe."

Tom looked from me to his father and then at the fish. The rainbow hues were already fading. A sudden revulsion at endless death and the destruction of vibrant color surged over me. I wanted to scream, "Put it back and stop this senseless murder" — but it was, I tried to reason, only a fish, and I remained silent.

Tommy must have felt my badly hidden and senseless reaction — he put the fish gently in the water where it floated

144

belly up. He continued with his fishing until he was distracted by a small painted turtle, which he finally captured and watched anxiously for the balance of the morning.

We swam in the cool, clear water, diving for pebbles which glistened in the golden net of sunshine on the bottom. We dabbled Polly's newly discovered toes in the pond and she gurgled ecstatically.

We watched a merganser, with her young riding on her back as she paddled leisurely among the reeds. The egret, tired of hunting frogs, unfolded its enormous wings and flapped majestically to the far shore.

The sun moved down the sky and we turned homeward.

I pushed open the door and heard the radio blaring. I also heard the sound of dripping water and followed it to its source. The living room ceiling was on the living room floor and clouds of steam were issuing from the broken hot water pipe which had caused the damage.

I was mad — hopping mad — and I strode into the living room in a red-hot fury.

Dad sat glued to the radio!

" Blast it! I've watched and taken care of this house and everybody in it for three years, four months, and one day, and on that one day I leave you to look after yourselves and what do you do? You listen to that condemned radio which I wish to heaven would bust a gasket, and you let the ceiling fall down! "

I guess my knots must have untied too quickly. Dad just looked at me.

" Well, it's my ceiling, isn't it? "

I stormed down cellar to turn off the water valve. Robert had already done it.

I fixed supper for the kids, got them into pajamas, and put them to bed.

Suddenly a wild yell issued from the Pine Room and feet pounded on the stairs. Dad had snatched Tommy from his

145

crib and was carrying him outdoors.

I looked around to see if the Pine Room ceiling had collapsed. It was intact, but the radio was screaming in triumph — " The Japanese have surrendered — this is it, folks — this is V–J Day."

The church bell began to ring wildly, whistles blew, car horns honked. I looked at the map with its little pins and before my eyes they turned to endless crosses, to stars of David, to heaps of earth unmarked, to bodies tossing just outside the breakers, and my heart cried out: " Be still, be quiet. Hush your screaming noise! " but someone took my hand and led me to the church and pointed.

There stood my father, his white hair ruffled, tears on his lined cheek where his own battle scar stood out clearly against the tan. His hands were on the bell rope, strong and sure, and Tommy in striped pajamas was clinging to the same strand.

Each time the heavy bell went over it jerked the small boy off his feet, and he laughed with the joy of a victory he could not understand.

I looked around at the others: Robert, the Duchess, Aunt Mary, Grandma Arny, Aunty Fern, and my own hands reached out to swing the bell faster.

In the catastrophic birth pangs of a new era, the dawn of the atomic age, the calm, sure hand of heaven moves at its unchanging pace, creating men to face and to solve the problems that their forebears have so neatly posed upon the squared-up board of life.

Our boarders did not depart with victory. Business was booming.

Reba was the youngest and the prettiest of all of our extra family. She was on the graveyard shift, so we saw very little of her, but when we did we loved her company; she was filled with laughter and knew endless stories, all of them really

146

funny. But as Christmas approached she became more and more reticent, and we saw her only as she came and went, wrapped in coveralls and a great coat with the collar turned up.

Since she had not eaten with us for weeks, I asked her if she didn't want to change the arrangements about her board, but she said she didn't, and would take a snack from the ice box with an easier conscience if we let things go along as they were. Since she was plump, and her color was excellent, I didn't pursue the matter any further, and at the end of the month I was glad I hadn't. Her consumption of " snacks " was enormous.

But on Christmas Eve, when all the rest were gathered around the tree singing carols and exchanging gifts, Reba did not appear. At first I thought that she was nursing a loneliness for her husband, overseas for more than a year, and could not bear the gaiety of the occasion, but the more I thought about it, the stranger her behavior seemed, and finally I went upstairs to get her.

I knocked on her door and was greeted by absolute silence. As I stood there, trying to decide whether or not to force the issue, I heard a peculiar sound, half moan, half sob, which was definitely not a cry of sorrow. There was only one place in the world where I had ever heard that particular combination of notes issuing from a human being, and I pushed the door open.

There was Reba, clutching the top of the bed, and trying not to cry aloud in labor.

It was obvious that there was not much time left for whatever action was necessary and I flew to the phone.

Don't ever be sick on Christmas Eve! Don't ever need a doctor! I phoned till I was hoarse, but 'twixt the still-filled Army rolls and the holiday, I could get no one. Not even the hospital had an available intern and the ambulance was out. They would send someone as soon as they could.

147

A quick mathematical count on the fingers showed the reason for Reba's reluctance to share her secret, but the secret was obviously about to announce itself, and that vocally. The cry of a newborn baby is unmistakable and cannot be hid.

There was nothing for it but for me to scrub, and quickly. Red Cross First Aid had not covered *this* emergency!

I have always suspected that the multifarious boiling of water in documentary films was simply a ruse to divert attention from the business at hand. Now I am sure of it. Clean sheets we had, thanks to Aunty Fern, and green soap was in plentiful supply. My lab coat I knew was reasonably sterile.

Reba was by this time cursing with a proficiency that I have never heard equaled, and though a moment of quiet evening prayer might have helped us through the business better, there was no time for it.

The infant's head had already presented itself. Reba labored and I worked. I expect that, according to all *lex* and mores, I should have been furious at her, and that, according to morality plays, the delivery should have been difficult. But I had only pity for her struggle, and her pain. From the fact that the baby arrived in less than half an hour, I gather that God has something better to do than to enforce humanity's standards on a girl in a sorry mess.

At last Reba was delivered, and she lay as still as death in a sleep deeper than any I have ever seen. I stood there with the baby wrapped in a receiving blanket, which I had snatched from our own nursery, when the calm voice of the Duchess spoke from behind me. " Did you tie the cord? " I nodded.

" Give me the baby, then go and comb your hair. Bring Reba some mulled wine from the hearth, and ask Robert for some for yourself."

" Duchess, this doesn't call for wine. What I need is a double brandy with aspirin."

The Duchess smiled as she rubbed oil on the baby. " How

many times have I told you that the one time not to take a drink is when you're sure you need one?" Then she laughed out loud, a joyful, friendly laugh: "And don't look so shocked. Neither you nor Reba, nor I, are responsible for the methods and procedures of reproduction in the human race. We did not invent them. It's a lovely baby and that is all that counts."

Reba stirred and looked at the Duchess.

"Why, you're not angry at all!"

"Why should I be?"

When, much later, combed and powdered and neat, I went downstairs, someone said: "This night is making me sentimental. I could have sworn I heard a baby cry."

"Sentimental, fidovolitz! You did. We just had one."

Jaws fell agape and they all looked at me as though I were an apparition. Suddenly it struck me funny, hilariously funny, and I managed to gasp: "Oh, Lord no! Not that! It's not my baby. I'm not *that* good! It's Reba's — it's a boy — drink up, everybody!"

For I had remembered that no one but the Duchess and I knew how long Reba's husband had been overseas, and there was no earthly reason why they ever should.

[19]

SPRING had come again, and the white mulberry tree spread its leaves above its soft golden trunk and its shade fell across the pool. It also fell across Mr. Slaight's rose bed when the sun moved north in the summer.

The punctilious landscape architect who had designed that proper garden had not made allowance for astronomical facts, an oversight that Mr. Slaight somehow rationalized as an intentional harassment on the part of the inhabitants of Tongue-

149

slip. The fact that the tree had made its full growth long before Mr. Slaight had made a rose bed was apparently irrelevant.

Dad and the Duchess, together with whatever friends and neighbors happened to be about at the time, had tea under its shade promptly at four o'clock on every pleasant day from April to October. Robins nested above them in the cover of the tree. Thrushes sang from its branches, and tanagers, plucking the succulent fruit, flashed their scarlet from its lowest limbs.

One summer we counted the visitors and found to our joy that sixty-nine species of birds ate, sang, or nested in the White Mulberry, which by this time had become capitalized in our minds and speech.

The tree was also perfect for climbing, and its structure was such that Tom could sit in the low crotch munching an apple and reading *Treasure Island* without imminent danger of falling out when, carried away by enthusiasm, he held up a pair of imaginary pistols and shouted, " One more step, Mr. Hands, and I'll blow out your brains! "

All these advantages were lost upon Mr. Slaight, who muttered that the tree dwarfed his house and, still bitter over the setback from Ganz and the bees, complained periodically that birds left droppings in his bath because of the laxative effects of the fruit. This, though not a genteel topic of conversation, is a matter that should be disposed of at once and for all. A bird bath cannot be kept pristine. Like any other modern convenience, it requires proper attention with a brush.

So far as I personally was concerned, I liked the White Mulberry Tree for reasons of laziness as well as of beauty. When it was in leaf there was no necessity for me to pull down the bedroom shades. It screened our windows from prying eyes and gave the sundeck a privacy not to be found elsewhere, except perhaps on a remote atoll, well outside the shipping lanes.

The little girls loved the tree even more than we did, because its drooping branches made an ideal hiding place, a heaven-sent dollhouse, cool and fragrant, and its leaves were ideal food for every caterpillar, woolly bear, or naked Luna larvae, which they collected and treated with tender consideration in return for the joy of watching cocoons in the making and the miraculous transfiguration that takes place on warm June nights when, with infinite labor, the bedraggled but metamorphosed moth emerges. Then we all stand spellbound watching the limp wings waver, and the gross body travail until its life blood flows into the myriad-colored wings, stretching them, smoothing them, strengthening them, until at last the lovely creature takes flight into the darkness and is gone from our knowledge.

To the Slaights of the world a moth is an insect to be sprayed with DDT, a curse to humanity, an eater of woolens. So much for categorical labels. But it is such generalized terms that rob them of so many happy experiences.

Tommy apparently sensed my confused hostility, for he invariably flung his apple cores into the mathematical center of the rose bed, and Mr. Slaight retaliated by heaving blue Bromo Seltzer bottles into our hedge.

In these exchanges I was always in the middle. Being still close enough to childhood to remember the bitterness of friendly advances slapped down ruthlessly, I knew that Tom's apple cores were in the nature of a defiant gauntlet, and yet I was old enough to have my heart ache for the Slaights, who would rather yank up fringed gentians by the roots than share their transient beauty with someone else.

What a dreadful fear of life one must have to resent the tree that may dwarf one's house! How deep must be despair when the art one admires is flung upon the canvas in sordid blacks, and patternless faces take on the green of corpses too long left unburied! What blows must have fallen upon the mind so to rock its foundations that the only escape from fate lies in the utter anonymity of thinking, dressing, building, and living in the plastic exactitude of the masses!

So I silently picked up the blue Bromo Seltzer bottles, which should in themselves have been a clue, and put them in the dustbin while Robert offered to help Mr. Slaight extend his rose bed to the south, and the Duchess took some choice hybrid teas to fill the extension. Both offers were met with curt refusal. Mr. Slaight wanted no sunny rose bed dug by friendly hands — he would not be beholden. If we would not take the mulberry to the woodpile, he would go without his roses, and that was that.

So he went without them, though he had a quarter of an acre of valley lilies in the broiling sun in which his seven cats meowed, rolled, rejoiced, and conceived kittens by the score.

Meanwhile, we at Tongueslip drank our tea, and inveigled the thrushes and chickadees to join the party and accept raisins out of the pound cake, from our hands.

As the year moved forward through the summer and fall, so those at Tongueslip aged with the almost imperceptible folding of a spruce in time of drought.

Where their steps had been straight forward and firm, they sometimes faltered, and each journey to the Plaza was frought with intense interest in a fallen leaf, an ant hill, or anything which gave excuse for pause.

Dad and the Duchess watched the garden with eagle eyes, and when the first black frost blighted the zinnias they made their reservations on the Silver Meteor and followed the birds south.

To this day it takes all that I have to go to the Pennsylvania Station. I always see someone there whose white hair blows back from his forehead as the great silver diesel roars past, and I hear myself saying, "God bless," and then the reply, "Amen."

And then I go out to the car, as I did on that day, and fight back my tears because not for all the tea in China would I confess to weakness. I have work to do. I must prune the White Mulberry.

I got out the tools and wandered down the border and stood speechless. Where once the tree had stood was — nothing.

A neat pile of logs, their bark golden brown in the sun of early winter, lay beside the stump of our beloved tree.

I pounded on the Slaights' back door and kicked it open with a savage thrust. The sharp pruning hook was in my hand, and I must have looked like an avenging fury. Mrs. Slaight stared at me from tear-rimmed eyes. She clutched a turkey drumstick and absently gnawed a piece of meat from the bone. Her hand shook.

" I'm sorry. I told him not to — but he is not — he is not well."

I saw the half empty bottle of bourbon on the sink, and everything fell into place — the blue Bromo Seltzer bottles, the sullen silences, the roaring brawls, the eternal calling of the cops, and I realized in one awful blinding flash that Mrs. Slaight — my childhood dragon — was scared to death of *me*.

I leaned the pruning hook in the corner, poured a cup of coffee from the stove, and shoved her gently back into her chair.

A cat rubbed against my legs and meowed.

I could have wrung its neck, but instead I talked to Mrs. Slaight while she finished the bone. We agreed that when Dad came back from Florida we would say the tree came down as the result of a storm. After all, it was a storm — after a fashion.

According to the best theories of fairy tales, life after this touching scene should have been one long, sweet, rosy dream. Maybe we don't live right, but there was no happy ending to this episode — in fact, everything went from bad to worse.

Mrs. Slaight's cats got into my banding traps and killed sixteen winter wrens at one clip. Mr. Slaight blazed away at Aluco's hole in the barn eaves. Tommy broke the Slaights' picture window with a well-aimed football and, like a lunkhead, I paid for the damage instead of suing the Slaights for the mulberry tree.

Christmas came and went, always a season of wonder and this year at least of peace. Armed truce in the wide world and in the little world of Slaight and Arny. When Mr. Slaight, to Robert's great annoyance, pulled up the stones that marked the boundary, armed truce grew into conscious tension.

What had gotten into everyone I cannot imagine, unless it was that Tongueslip's pet ghost went on a rampage. We have one of course. He never does anything more annoying than sneezing violently in the middle of the night unless it is that he constantly hides things where we cannot find them. Anyhow, on New Year's Eve he knocked the mirror above the mantel off the wall. It came down with a resounding crash, smashed my choice red lacquer vases to smithereens, and came to rest on the stone hearth intact.

Perhaps our ghost only wanted to hex us, for had the glass smashed, it could have meant seven years of bad luck.

It's a good thing we didn't get that! One year of the jinx's hex was all I could hope to survive!

In fact, even now there is very little about it that strikes me as being at all funny. It did, however, teach me the value of prayer. Praying serves a very practical purpose. It slows us down, gives us time to think before we react, and therefore unquestionably does make things turn out better regardless of the divinity of the intervention.

New Year's Day there was a blizzard. Snow fell in fine flakes and powdered the lawn with the myriad miracles of differing loveliness that will always remain incredible to me. For the first day it was beautiful. By the time it had reached the doorsteps and begun to filter over the threshold and into the house it had lost some of its charm. When it reached the window ledges it had become " that damn stuff."

The children were possessed to go out and play in it, and very unwisely I let them. I watched out the window as they floundered and made angels and wondered idly how deep the drifts were. Suddenly Polly disappeared. I waited for her to stand up and she didn't. It took no great intelligence to realize that if she stayed under "that stuff" long she would smother, so I went after her. As I approached the drift from the house side, I went in to the hips and then to the waist, but finally I managed to reach her and pick her up in my arms. I tried to turn and could not. By a slow scuffling and shifting I managed to get around so that I was facing the house. To call for help was fruitless. Neither Tommy nor Aunt Mary, nor Aunty Fern, could do anything against that bitter cold and wind, and the snow had begun to swirl again so that none of the neighbors could see me.

You feel like a fool trapped in an inanimate drift in your own back yard and in imminent danger of freezing to death. It had never occurred to me to put on a coat. It had looked so simple.

Step by step I slogged toward the edge of the drift. Polly gained weight with every second. No sooner did I make room for my legs to inch forward than the snow fell into it like sand into a child's well at the seashore.

Panic, sheer and unadulterated, grabbed me by the throat, and then fury. Of all the putrid ways to die! Of all the stupid ways to die! Of all the ignominious ways to die this took the bun, and I was darned if I was going to freeze to death in the rose bed. Adrenalin poured, and with it came a surge of energy that landed me flat on my back with Polly on top of me at the edge of the drift. I couldn't get up!

I swam out of that drift with one hand and thrashing feet. My language melted the snow in front of me I think, and Polly was able to help by digging her heels against the rose-bushes.

Finally we were on the level and I got her to the house, where I turned around and gave her what for, as only an adult who has been a complete jackass in the first place *can* give it to a child. In this respect I find it diverting that the gestation period of a jackass is 380 days and of a human being 280. This choice gem of useless information intrigues me with its philosophical possibilities. Anyway, the next day it rained. As it rained it froze. The trees sagged, and by nightfall the wires had begun to come down. They lashed across the glittering ice and shorted. The smell of ozone and the arcing of sparks filled the air. The night was brilliant with blue flashes and sharp cracks.

Then the trees began to go. They exploded with a crash like the crack of doom, and fell with the sound of a multitude tearing crisp paper. My conscience screamed, You asked for it — here's the storm — you won't have to lie about the Mulberry Tree — are you satisfied?

The lights were out. The oil burner was off and then the gas line froze. This, of course, made it highly likely that the pipes would freeze, so we had to drain all the plumbing. If a pipe bursts at Tongueslip, you have to go through a three-foot stone wall to fix it. We avoid that when possible.

Bob and Tommy chopped and sawed all day to keep enough wood in the fireplaces for cooking and survival. There was no point in yelling to our friends — they were all in the same boat — that is, for three days.

On the fourth day everybody else had power and heat. We didn't. We had tried to be patient, realizing that the linemen were exhausted, but patience wears thin when you have had no sleep and cooked over a wood fire for days. Finally Robert exploded. He told the power company that if we did not get our juice in eight hours, he would go up the pole himself and put in a jumper. The linemen came. It was then that we discovered that the last man up the pole had forgotten to replace the door fuse, and we might as well have had our power for the previous three days. Next time I shall yell louder and sooner!

That was not the end for the year of the blizzard. Things

156

smoothed out, but only for a while. True, we knew that the older members of the family had been living on borrowed time for years, but we hardly thought that all notes would be called in at once. When Aunty Fern fell ill, and neither skill nor love could save her, we were desolate.

Soon afterward Aunt Mary began to complain of feeling drowsy. Her sleeps lengthened and lengthened until one afternoon, as I sat beside her reading, she slipped across the border from sleep to final rest.

Her affairs were not yet settled when I received a phone call from the Duchess, telling me that Dad was very ill and I was to take the next plane to Florida. Before I got my suitcase packed, Robert was home from the plant with the final news that Dad had already gone to the happy hunting grounds.

At this point in the tale of Tongueslip, I shall probably be roundly censured by some as being completely lacking in any sense of propriety, but there will be others who will understand. Perhaps Dad's greatest legacy to me was an incorrigible sense of humor, and I know he would have enjoyed the joke more than any of us. I cannot deprive him of his last laugh. As I said, Aunt Mary's affairs were not yet settled, and, as luck would have it, the cemetery lot was in her name. She had arranged to will it to me and had written a letter to that effect. When I called to have Dad's grave opened, the squisley little man at the cemetery said pompously, " On whose authority? " I told him on mine. He flatly refused to open the grave without Aunt Mary's signature.

Seeking to be both reasonable and courteous, I drove to the cemetery armed with Aunt Mary's letter and the surrogate's certificate. Mr. Squeam took one look at the documents stating in Aunt Mary's own hand that the lot was to be mine, and bellowed: " This letter was written before she died. It would not hold up in court." To which I answered, in a voice which I dare say was caustic beyond necessity: " And, sir, when did you expect her to write the letter? After she was dead? "

He still refused to open the grave. Time was getting on. The service was the next day at noon, and in cold weather the earth has to be artificially thawed for the sextons. I glared across the desk in my best D.A.R. manner and told Mr. Squeam that he had better have that grave open in the morning, and if he didn't, I should most certainly come up and dig it myself. It was a pretty pass indeed if a man could not lie in his own grave without an order from the court! Mr. Squeam was evidently impressed. I came back two hours later and found the sextons at work.

Mother arrived on the train completely exhausted and lacking any decent black for the service.

Miss McNamarra, who had always seen to the impeccable wardrobe of the Duchess, was on hand. She started to pin yards of black crepe to Mother's hat, and the Duchess said quite simply, " Thank you, McNamarra, I don't want anything like that," to which McNamarra replied, through a mouthful of pins, " Come along now, dearie — it's so smart, so becoming, so fashionable, and you don't know when you'll ever have a chance to wear it again."

For a moment I saw Dad standing in the room in his tar-smeared, tattered coveralls, and he was holding onto his sides and rocking with laughter. The Duchess must have seen him too, for the two of us laughed together as we have seldom laughed before, and I for one am glad — glad from the bottom of my heart — that the last glimpse I had of the parson of Tongueslip was a rollicking, delighted, laughing glimpse of a man who could find something funny in his own widow's weeds.

[20]

WE SAT by the fire at Tongueslip and tried to pull ourselves together. I remember very little about those weeks except that someone said to me, "Please stop looking like a wooden Indian."

I *felt* like a wooden Indian. My tepee was very, very empty. There were also practical considerations. Tongueslip is large and requires much wampum for heating. Let it go at that — we had to retrench. The north end of the house is complete in itself. The archway could be closed. We closed it, and rented our salubrious front banisters for the edification of somebody who could afford the luxury of sliding down them.

For the first time the dinner table was set for six, and when I looked at it, I knew that there was something definitely out of order. Then I saw what was wrong. My napkin ring was at the end of the table where Mother's had always been.

I started to move it to its proper place. The Duchess spoke quietly: "Leave it there, Mary. I think it best that we all understand that you and Robert belong in our places now."

It was that episode which made me understand completely why young Elizabeth's earrings wobbled so precariously when she was lifted into King Edward's chair.

To become mistress of Tongueslip implied a responsibility. The Duchess was married in satin slippers, size 2. My own 7-B's can never adequately fill them.

If the Duchess crosses the main drag, traffic stops to let her pass. If I pause to look up at a flight of wild geese, someone on a kiddie car is sure to bump my shins.

Robert, on the other hand, bids fair to become this generation's Deacon Martin. Everyone loves him, everyone trusts him, everyone turns to him for help. It comforts me to know that as the years go on we shall retain at least a vestige of respecta-

159

bility. Particularly when I think of what happened next!

The thawing ice betrayed the carnage wrought by storm. Lilacs split asunder, azaleas shattered, trees decapitated and dying had to be cleared away. All over town crews of men went to work. It was a seemingly endless task, and they were still at it late in the spring.

I've explained before that I'm a congenital sidewalk engineer, and the trees that were bowing to ax and saw offered limitless possibilities. Miss Grissing, who was Tom's teacher at the time, told him about a maple on Cooper Avenue that looked promising, and we went up there immediately. It was the Bishops' tree, and Mr. Bishop had made the discovery that there was a nest in the fallen trunk. The buzz saws had missed it by scarcely an inch, but missed it they had.

Madam Otis Asio Otis, known to her intimates as a screech owl, lay stiff and very dead in her Cooper Avenue residence. Under her were four small white objects which appeared to be slightly dirty marshmallows.

John and Peter Hughes rescued nest and babies and took Madam O. A. Otis along for taxidermy purposes.

Tommy and I looked longingly at the owl family and Judge Trimble came over to see what was what. Miss Grissing had evidently spoken kindly of us. The boys and the Judge went into a huddle. Out of it came a verdict which changed life at Tongueslip for all time to come.

John and Peter Hughes relinquished their rights, in the matter of the owls, to us graciously and cheerfully. We put, nest, corpse, and babies in the car and took off for home.

No sooner were we in the house than we discovered how wrong a diagnosis can be. Madam Otis shot out of the nest, landed on the frame of Dad's portrait, and expressed her opinion of us and our forebears in unmistakable terms.

What does one do with a furious owl? Cousin Betty, the one whom we visited at Cuttyhunk when we encountered the runaway horse, was visiting us at the time. I don't know

160

how she achieves it, but she is I think the only person I have ever known whose one thought, always, is to make other people happy and comfortable. The Duchess says that Mrs. Grover Cleveland was the same way.

Betty's instinct for courtesy extended to the owls. She remembered my story about the egg at the hospital and wondered if Mac was still there.

She was, and the "eminent ornithologist" was waiting to take her home. D'Arcy and Mac would stop in about the owls on their way.

I have never seen a neater piece of work than d'Arcy's fielding of that owl. He whistled a funny little tune, walked over, and picked her off the portrait without ruffling a feather. I shook my head in wonder.

"D'Arcy, I though she was dead. She was stiff and had her eyes closed! Then when we got in here, she just took off."

"Lots of creatures feign death; it is not at all confined to possums."

"Now what do we do?"

"You might see if she will hunt for her young and feed them. Have you a board about? I'll make a roof for the nest and we can try it in a likely spot. It's a thin chance but worth it."

Tommy got a board and a saw. Robert walked in about then and he and d'Arcy set up the nest on the porch roof.

Polly looked at it a minute and went out to the goosehouse, whence she returned with a straw.

"How you going to know if the sowl comes back?"

Well, how were we? She had taken off in an awful hurry, and if we sat with a light on the nest entrance waiting for her, she would be even more reluctant to return.

Polly leaned the straw in the opening. "There! If she goes in, the straw will fall out, see?"

We saw.

"If she doesn't come back by ten tonight, you'd better feed

them." D'Arcy looked at me dubiously. "They eat mice, you know – their weight in mice every day."

We ate our own dinner of hamburger, and I for one hoped that Mrs. "Sowl" *would* come back, but at half past ten she hadn't.

The Arnys had taken her children in; the Arnys could jolly well raise them.

The nearest thing we had to a mouse was the remnants of our dinner. I warmed some chopped beef in my hand to feed the owlets. But how much should I feed them? Their weight! We got out the letter scales and carefully determined the fact that they could go first-class mail for three cents each. That was some criterion to go by, and at least the owlets would open their mouths, which is more than can be said for most wild foundlings.

They didn't eat, they just wrapped themselves around the hamburger in great hunching gulps and then backed to the edge of the nest and evacuated. Well, I knew that anyhow. They could be housebroken. Their instinct was to keep their home clean.

We went to bed – Robert with the controlled crinkle at the corners of his eyes that indicate that he is convinced more than ever that I am completely mad, but loves me just the same.

I started counting mice. One mouse a day to begin with, more as the babies grew. I felt like Alice as she went down the rabbit hole.

"One mouse times four is four mice, times seven is twenty-eight mice, times fifty-two – that is too complicated – times ten is two hundred eighty, times five is one thousand and four hundred, which is too many mice, and I won't bother about the extra two weeks, for there just aren't that many mice. I'll have to find something else."

Find it we did. Fur or feathers are essential to the diet of owls. We got an old pillow and snipped the feathers into small bits, and mixed in the chopped meat and fed the owlets; occasionally we added ground-up bones.

The owlets throve. But something was radically wrong with *us*. We itched. We tried to scratch politely and inconspicuously, but there was no hiding it. Finally the Duchess allowed that she had not itched like that since she had had fleas in Italy. Fleas! I looked the owlets over — the itching was explained.

We Pulvexed the owlets. We Flitted the furniture, we vacuumed the rugs, and we washed ourselves and our hair with dog soap. The odor was not ethereal, but the itching ceased.

The next day the four owlets opened their eyes. They were a cloudy blue, and fixed upon us with an intent gaze. The eye of the owl is a wondrous thing. It can focus close like a microscope and far like a telescope. It is never still. The pupil dilates and contracts with every shift of light. Owls *can* see in the daytime but they see even better at night. Some say that they are like snooperscopes, sensitive to infrared, and that is why they can locate living prey in the pitch-black dark of midnight. To me their sight is a miracle. I have never been able to understand why people are so awed by the restoring of sight to the blind beggar in Galilee. To me the real miracle is that we *all* see. Birds, beasts, men are given eyes, intricate, wonderful, beyond belief — a free gift from the Giver of life — and of all these eyes, the owls' are the most amazing.

Slowly they turned from blue to amber, and by this time our house guests were about four inches high. Small ear tufts were definitely in evidence. Their appetites increased in proportion to their size. The University lab offered to send us mice.

This generous offer I rejected. I am a woman with a strong stomach, but it balks at drowning ten mice a day. The meat and pillow stuffings were quite adequate.

After some three weeks of meat, feathers, and sitting on the mantelpiece ogling us, the owlets decided to take to the air.

The wonder to us was how they knew what to do. They had their eyes closed when we got them and they'd never seen a bird since, but they took off in an echelon and made a perfect three-point landing on top of the corner cupboard.

Then the fun *really* began. Chattering and burbling, they seized the basket of keys thereon and threw them to the floor. They swooped, they circled, they stole all my pencils and chewed them to shreds.

Not content with this, they rode the turntable of the Victrola like kids at Coney Island and sat on the carriage of the typewriter, grabbing at the flying keys.

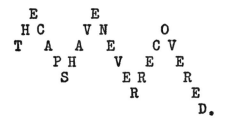

Their favorite perch was in the fanlight over the door, and one evening when Robert was trying to get them down, our new minister, Dell Buttrey, came to call. Bob was standing on a chair in front of the door and shouted, "Just a minute till I get these owls down!"

It's lucky for us that Dell has a priceless sense of humor. I think most clergymen would smell the breath of a deacon who was picking owls!

Mary K. said the owls were like kittens with feathers. The description is apt. They sat on our shoulders, burbling and rubbing their soft heads against our cheeks, and they were as careful with their sharp talons as a gentle pussy with her claws.

All went well until the Sunday supplement gave the orphan owls a full-page spread. Then all hope of peace departed.

There had not been so much excitement since Dad rode a

164

wild bull moose on a bet. Tongueslip became as private as the Grand Central Station. "If only," said the Duchess, "we had charged admission, we could all retire!"

The owlets strode up and down the mantle like Bligh on his quarter-deck. Their stance was suggestive of hands under coattails. When a visiting admiral called to inspect them, the owls went into conference and started what we called "the owling act."

Their bodies remained perfectly still, but their heads went round like human being watching midget auto races on television. They were impressed no end by gold braid, so I guess they really aren't so wise after all.

People kept telling us how dangerous it was for us to keep these owlets with their "evil eye." Surely we knew that owls' calling meant death, that they could only be stopped from screeching by pointing a shoe at a church.

On this matter I humbly present the evidence.

First, for the only time in twenty years no one died, or was ill, within the parish, or the family, during the period that we had the owls. This is in itself a minor miracle. Secondly, the shoe proposition was tested with extreme and scientific accuracy. We took a shoe from each member of the family. We took Malvina's shoe, and we borrowed a shoe from the Changs, and we lined our own shoes up in a neat row. When the owls started to screech, we pointed them toward the church. There was no lessening of the noise.

Then we opened the window and put the shoes beside the church and listened carefully. The owls continued to call. We next arranged a system of light signals, which could be seen by all concerned, and set the shoes on the porch of the church. The song increased in intensity. Inside the church the same thing happened.

I doubt if any combination of science and religion could have been more thorough, and trust that the experiment was recorded with amusement by Saint Peter, for in a way it was a contribution. It may be categorically stated that no shoe, right or left, new or old, belonging to any specific sex, race, color, or creed, will, when placed in any position relative to a church, even on the high altar, stop a screech owl from screeching.

That is one ghost of fear and trembling laid, by the happy juxtaposition of a naturalist, a liberal clergyman, and a church. So much for the working together of science and religion.

[21]

EVENTUALLY the owlets reached maturity and were released. This was in June, and so they can in no wise be held accountable for the events of the following February.

We should have known, all of us, that presenting a Spartan front to the public and trying to behave as though nothing at all had happened in the family at Tongueslip was folly.

Nobody can go through a prolonged siege of illness and deaths and sorrow with complete immunity. One thinks the head can outsmart the heart, but this is a profound fallacy. Something has to give.

Mary Katharine came down with a beautiful case of pneumonia; Tommy and Polly followed in her train. I, of course, was invincible. I could handle everything. In about three weeks I learned better. I too succumbed. Having stated before that Mac saved my bacon, I suppose that this is the point at which to explain it, although I have not the slightest intention of giving a blow by blow description of the entire era of debacle.

Suffice it to say that when " Mary the Mighty " was laid low, she selected a day when the snow was filtering in over the window sills and nobody could get a car out of a driveway.

Sally and Don Pratt, who live across the street, and to whom I turn in every moment of crisis because they stand like Gibralter in a stormy sea, had a cylinder of oxygen which they keep on hand for Don's mother, who is somewhere in the vicinity of the century mark. They lent it to Bob for me. It was a gadget with which Bob was not familiar. Dr. Stella Bradford could not sit there all night and work it. She, being well along in years and a woman of sterling worth, was able to get to Tongueslip, but only I am sure because her guardian angel is so used to her unconquerable soul that he never lets any material obstacle stop her. Be that as it may, Mac and Aunt Stella, by dint of love, managed to make it through the drifts; cash had not been a sufficient inducement to anybody else. I got through that night anyhow.

This unpleasant business of illness is very rough on a family, and before many days the Duchess and Robert also had a goodly dose of the germ. Tongueslip became a hospital, with regular shifts of medical and domestic personnel. If I could remember what happened, I would make a long and loving list of friends, but Sophia Conover was the last one whose helpful presence penetrated my foggy semiconsciousness. Since none of us have ever indulged in half measures, we kept the neighborhood in a constant state of dither and the undertaker in a constant state of anticipation for some time.

When, afterwards, it was fairly certain that we would none of us become subjects for the obituary column, the Duchess and I were removed to the hospital, and there I remained in solitary grandeur for over a month, unaware of Robert's illness. During this period, since there was nothing else to do, I had a splendid opportunity to observe and to ponder.

By now it should be evident that we are not a sanctimonious family sitting in a holier-than-thou ecclesiastical cloud and dropping pearls of wisdom before our inferiors, so perhaps it will not be taken amiss if I try to share a philosophy of life that helps me over the inevitable bumps.

In a hospital one encounters humanity at its best and at its worst. I am not now, and was not then, particularly concerned about people with a routine appendectomy who can find nothing better to do than to keep three special nurses dancing and complain about the curve of the spoons. Nevertheless, they set me to thinking, when I contrasted them with some of the patients who really had something to cry about. For what they are worth, I came to a few conclusions. Not of course quite as simply as that; In fact, I remember Mac standing in my room one spring midnight and saying, "When it is dark enough, you will be able to see the stars."

It is terribly easy to say, "Why did God do this to *me?*"

It is so terribly hard to remember that you are not the end all and be all of creation. There are few people who at one time or another have not asked that question, and I keep hoping that perhaps my trek down the trail of wondering will help them, even before the darkness falls.

What is it all about, this little span of years? Why do we live, and suffer, and bear grief, and work, and die? Is it all some colossal joke at which the gods are laughing, or is there some purpose, some way of life?

Book religion isn't very helpful when the only thing in the world that matters is to escape from the burden. Somehow the intellect demands that the soul hang on, if only by the fingernails, until creation makes sense. And so, I turned the kaleidoscope of life, seeking a pattern.

Theoretically I should be a good Christian. I have certainly been exposed to all that men know about our faith. But, I admit it, "It is God's will" never satisfied me for an answer.

Some of the things that befall in this world certainly are *not* the whim and fancy of the God I was raised to love and respect. My interest has always lain in life, not in death. I am a natural scientist. Can I, in my extremity, find a relationship between the faith of my fathers and the facts that I have ob-

168

served? I think I can. I know that if I am to live and remain sane I must.

Naturally, being a Christian, one tends to think in terms of Jesus. If one can accept orthodoxy, the problem is simple. But can one, really? The scientist is trained in the observation of facts, and from them he draws his conclusions. Can the search for God be reduced to experimental terms? Hardly. Therefore one must turn to the authority, and to me the authority is the Nazarene. If anybody ever understood what it was all about, He did. But how — how?

A fragment of the sayings from the Oxyrhynchus papyrus, found in Egypt by the joint expedition of Oxford and the University of Pennsylvania, gives Jesus' own answer, in his own words:

"Ye ask who are those that draw us to the kingdom, if the kingdom is in heaven. . . . The fowls of the air, and all the beasts that are under the earth, or upon the earth, and all the fishes of the sea, these are they which draw you, and the kingdom of heaven is within you; and whosoever shall know himself, shall find it. Strive therefore to know yourself, and ye shall be aware that ye are the sons of the Almighty Father, and ye shall know that ye are in the city of God and ye are the city."

It is not easy to lie in the white sterility of a hospital and objectively know yourself, so I conjured up the pine forest and its denizens. It can be done! I am told that the technique is a familiar one to convicts, and if so I am glad that they are thus able to escape with their minds at least. I, like any stir-crazy prisoner, mentally retreated to the woods, and sought the birds and the beasts.

Surely to do this is not theologically unreliable, for the fact is abundantly clear that Jesus himself haunted the woods and the fields and sat in thought beside the waters of Galilee. In this respect all the Gospels agree. Jesus of Nazareth was undoubtedly an interested and competent Naturalist. Moreover,

169

He used the plants and the birds and the animals consistently in His parables. One feels no incongruity in following such a precedent.

And so one considers the mountain laurel, Kalmia latifolia, also known as the calico bush. In May and June it is in full sway. It covers the hillsides and overflows into woodlands and gardens. Its star-shaped flowers fill the air with an elusive fragrance which is usually overwhelmed by the heavy sweetness of honeysuckle. Bees hum around its myriad blossoms, and fledglings perch precariously on its russet twigs.

Each cluster of blooms is made up of some fifty blossoms, cunningly equipped with a mechanism delicate beyond belief, which insures the survival of this miracle of loveliness.

The stamens of the mountain laurel are ten in number, and each stamen is tucked into a minute pocket at the side of the blossom. The anthers, filled with pollen, are crimson-lake in color, as it is they which, by sheer force of numbers, create an illusion of pinkness.

Ten stamens in each blossom; fifty blossoms on each cluster; as many as a hundred clusters on a single average-sized plant. This is a phenomenal creation in itself, for, to put it on an easily envisaged basis, there are on the average mountain laurel more blossoms than there are visible stars in the sky on the crispest of August nights, and there are in each blossom ten stamens.

Now comes the incredible fact. Each of these myriad pollen-bearing sacs is balanced so delicately in its place that the weight of the bee, visiting the flower in search of nectar, releases the filament and sends the stamen into a reverse curve which strikes the bee neatly on its fuzzy back and inundates it with pollen. Not only does it do this, but it entangles her so that when she struggles to free herself, the other stamens also arise, and likewise shower her with the life-giving substance.

And then what? Then the bee goes to another blossom, still

170

in search of nectar. The pollen on her back adheres to the sticky stigma and starts to grow. The grain of pollen now near to the unfertilized egg of the plant grows rapidly, and eventually joins with the seed-forming cells of the laurel, causes them to become fertile, to ripen and mature, and finally to fall from the parent plant to the earth beneath. There the seed germinates.

So it happens that the mountain laurel covers the hillsides, overflows into woodlands and gardens. Its blossoms outnumber the stars, and this vast blooming of the countryside is set in motion by the weight of a worker bee. Tell me, then, what is unimportant?

Certainly the plan for the laurel is a plan of life and of living. Such ingenuity was not exercised to support death in his seemingly endless forays against all beauty.

A wedge of wild geese honked over in the lonely hours before dawn, and I wondered at the great mystery of migration. Why do the birds go south, or north, and know how to go, and where? Is there a long-remembered journey? Scientists do not know why birds migrate. There is no reason why they should. They could for the most part find ample food and shelter if they simply stayed on their wintering grounds. But, instead, they undertake a journey — a long, hard journey.

The golden plover is a small bird, about the size of a bantam rooster. It breeds on the arctic tundra. Its beauty is breathtaking, black beneath the golden above. It moves on dainty feet across the sphagnum moss, lays its eggs, incubates them, and hatches its young.

But in winter can it live in the arctic? It cannot. There is no food. So what is the provision made for it? It takes flight over the Rockies and the High Sierra. Some plovers go to the pampas of South America, but others do something infinitely more remarkable.

They beat their way to the shores of the rolling Pacific, and there dance along the edge of the waves, gathering food and

171

strength. Then, with surging wings, these small creatures take to the air, and plow across the boundless ocean in a direct line to the Hawaiian Islands.

Three thousand miles of open ocean, nonstop; one fueling at the shore of the Pacific, and then the beating of wings across uncharted seas where there is no possible landmark!

Buffeted by storms, blown by the wind, they go, straight as a die to the warm climate where there is food, the means of life.

Here in God's plan again there is the fulfillment of the desire for life, and Jesus said that He had come that we might have life and have it more abundantly.

Well, what then of the "lower" animals that Reinhold Niebuhr says have no individuality, no soul? I wish Mr. Niebuhr had known our owls. Then he would be better qualified to talk about God's creatures. Salar the salmon is one of these that men look down upon as unimportant. Yet does nature fail him?

Far up the Tobique and the Miramichi, Salar moves his silver scales. Men fish for him with more or less success; indeed, this naturalist recalls being pulled into a pool in the Tobique up to her waist by one of Salar's cousin's. They are a mighty breed, and wise.

Salar's children are called "parr," and they live in the rivers until they are two years old; then, for some reason best known to them, but said to be a memory of a long-ago journey, they go down to the sea.

Where they go no man knows, but there they stay until they become grilse, old enough to breed.

All the salmon of the Western Hemisphere go to the broad Atlantic, and all the salmon stay there feeding and growing. Then the life surge takes them back, back from the chasms of the ocean, back along the coast. Each goes to his own river, each goes to his own continent, each goes to his own country.

Race after race surges up the river. Leaping and jumping,

flashing silver in the sunlight above the white water of the rapids, twisting and turning at the base of the falls, and then surging and fighting the torrent, they beat their way up the roaring cataract, swimming almost vertically, pounded and beaten until their bodies show red where the scales have been torn loose in the battle. Salar the salmon comes to rest in his pool.

There his mate deposits her eggs, and there Salar swims back and forth spilling his white milt upon them, giving them life. The young hatch. Salar and his mate depart about their own business. The parr stay in the river for two years and then, never having known their parents, never having been told the way, never having felt the salt sea in their gills, they turn downstream, back to the sea, down through the white waters, over the brink of the falls, out to the broad Atlantic.

Never do they lose their way. Never does an American salmon go to England; never does a salmon from the Highlands enter the mouth of the Tobique. Why? Has the water a different taste? Or could it be something else that their instinct never leads them astray, never urges them toward life and then betrays them? Instinct? Or is there a shorter word, God?

Leaping and surging up the rivers of the North the salmon run. Salar's children from the Highlands, and from the Fiords, from the rivers of Canada and America, Scotland and Germany. From the rivers of Scandinavia, from the rivers of England. Down to the sea, down to the sea and back. Dependable, always to the right river, always to create life.

It must have grown suddenly cold, for I found myself again on the tundra where I have not been for twenty years. I watched the lemmings playing, nuzzling each other, jumping about in what seemed to be aimless and pointless games, enjoying life and seeking nothing from it.

Suddenly, and for no apparent reason, they started to mill and to gather. One of them, not visibly wiser or stronger or bigger than the rest, began to move away from the crowd, seeking perhaps some independence. The rest of the pack followed him, and the faster he ran the faster they followed.

Their eyes seemed fixed on his rump, and they pelted across the lichens and mosses toward the bay. Obviously they were not seeking nests, for there was no rutting. They simply followed the leader blindly, inanely, unthinking, and without purpose, right into the icy waters of the bay.

There they struggled, and swam, and drowned. There was no purpose to their living, no purpose to their dying. They had selected a leader simply because he was the first to start off, and had never paused to inquire into the way or the direction in which he was leading them. They had achieved nothing but *Lebensraum* for those who were lagging behind, and destruction for those who followed the fastest. They consummated their own destruction, and as a by-product filled the bellies of the predators on land and in the sea.

There is indeed much that we may learn from ancient instruction. " The heavens declare the glory of God; and the firmament showeth his handiwork. . . . There is no speech nor language, where their voice is not heard. Their line is gone out through all the earth, and their words to the end of the world."

" Ye ask who are those that draw us to the kingdom, if the kingdom is in heaven. . . . The fowls of the air, and all the beasts that are under the earth, or upon the earth, and all the fishes of the sea, these are they which draw you." This indeed is the Scripture written by the Creator himself, as the psalmist says, and as Jesus says, legible to all men of all nations, even unto the ends of the earth. This Scripture is the original manuscript of the Great Author, and to me it clearly states that those creatures, those things endowed with the miracle of life, which go forth into that life with a purpose attain that purpose; that those who follow blindly in a surging, unthinking mass achieve nothing but their own destruction.

174

If a man, like the laurel, the golden plover, the tern, and Salar the salmon, is willing to battle the storms and vicissitudes of life for the sake of integrity, for the sake of creativity, for the sake of his progeny, he will arrive at the appointed place, for the appointed purpose, at the appointed time.

For if there is one certain thing in the universe it is that though the individual man, the individual plover, the individual salmon may fall victim to violence, to greed, or to selfishness, there still exists the overwhelming force of nature, which has always followed and will always follow and enforce the fundamental law of the universe, that that which is worthy of survival will survive.

[22]

THERE were other things besides a reasonable philosophy of life that I garnered from the hospital.

One of the favorite caustic comments at Tongueslip is, "You ought to have your head examined!"

For what it is worth, and I assure you that it was worth plenty, *my* head has been examined by the most eminent neurosurgeon in this area.

For no better reason than that I am careless, and prone to drop my silver while eating, comes this expert and pricks my arm with pins! But in the end, after exhaustive X-rays, tests, cotton wool on the eyeballs, etc., etc., he wrote on my chart, for the edification of anyone who is suspicious of my sanity, that I am a perfectly reasonable and rational human being, and testified thereby that there is nothing whatever the matter with my head, not even a suggestion of a crack. This comforts the family when I absent-mindedly put butter in my tea.

I remember distinctly the first time that my fork clattered

to the floor. It was at a very formal reception held by one of the local lion hunters. The old Doc came strolling up to the Duchess, prescription pad in hand. "Mary, you're a close friend of Ava's, perhaps you can give me her summer address. Deacon Martin wants it."

Since to our certain knowledge he had been sitting on Miss Ava's porch in the country on the previous afternoon, I dropped my fork!

The Duchess, with perfect aplomb, took the prescription pad and inscribed the address upon its pristine surface.

The old Doc bowed blandly and rejoined Deacon Martin. I nearly choked.

"Mother, for the love of Mike! That was a very touching tribute to your discretion, but he knows that address perfectly well. He's there every day!"

"My dear, when you are as old as he is, you will know enough not to cast a shadow of doubt across a friendship that is as wholesome as baked potatoes and could be as easily mashed by a single wagging tongue."

When we told Miss Ava about the incident, she laughed, "Why didn't you just write 'Rats'?"

Only once did the Duchess approach that suggested attitude with the old Doc. He had left her some medicine with the caution that it was highly potent and might react unfavorably on her rather touchy heart. He would, he said, be back that afternoon.

He was. He strolled into the middle room, sat down at the piano, played the "Unfinished Symphony" superbly and movingly, and walked out without even speaking to any of us.

A week later he called again and shouted up the stairs, "How's Mary?"

Dad winked at Mother. "I'm sorry, John, I forgot to call you. She died last Tuesday."

The old Doc was up those stairs in nothing flat! What do you do with a guy like that, except love him?

176

If anyone was really sick, he was a genius, infallible, eternally on the job, but let it be something trivial or, even worse, uninteresting, and that's the way he ticked! He's been dead a long time now, but he still is making legend.

I always chuckle when people look pityingly at the inhabitants of the parsonage and say: "Your life is so calm and peaceful. I should think you'd long for a little excitement once in a while — you know, something dramatic like that breathing tube the old Doc slid in with a razor blade!" Well, the old Doc certainly supplied us with drama and then some.

Tracheotomies are the good old ham theater stand-by. What happens in the life of a minister can't be filmed or published in the paper.

In fact, one of the parson's chief jobs is seeing that when some poor devil gets himself into a sorry mess neither the press nor the parish *does* hear about it. There was never a falser statement than that the large preponderance of clergymen's children listed in *Who's Who* is due to a calm and secure home life! A parsonage is constant bedlam.

Let some poor fellow hang himself from the rafters, and the preacher is called before the doctor and has the delicate task of placating the press without saying anything. Let a family descend to violence, and the preacher is called by the neighbors to prevent murder. Let anyone be drunk, and the preacher is called to make black coffee.

If any man should be able to put feeling into the words, "From battle and murder, and from sudden death, good Lord, deliver us!" it is the preacher who reads the petition. He has not only a spiritual, but also a very practical, reason for wishing to remain uninvolved. Those who have made monkeys of themselves are thereafter embarrassed, and remove themselves from the congregation, which makes helping them a discouraging proposition at best! If I were looking for a minister, I think I would choose the fellow who had lost the most members in the past year. He has probably helped them all out of

177

scandalous situations!

Habit is strong upon humanity. The parson no longer lives at Tongueslip, but disaster turns their footsteps usward still. We would not have it otherwise. Let a cat have kittens on the living room sofa, and the phone at Tongueslip clangs for attention. Calm indeed! Perfect peace! RATS!

The police likewise gravitate in our direction. Many's the time we have returned from a movie or a meeting to find a squad car parked in front of the house with a pigeon or possum under protective custody. Once, indeed, the desk sergeant sent me a beautiful Luna moth. No doubt the Ladies' Aid, who were playing bridge at our house that day, were surprised to see a six-foot-four patrolman carrying that exquisitely dainty creature into our parlor. But I appreciated that gift and thought more than I can ever say.

Maybe the desk sergeant remembered the story of Detective Colson and the skull. We of course are quite inured to shock, but, as a young man starting out, he must have been a bit jolted.

A visit from the Homicide Squad would, I think, give anybody pause. The weather was just right for it, bitter cold, howling wind, lowering clouds at the northeast, and Detective Colson standing at the door with the cheering announcement, "I'm from Homicide, and I've been looking for you."

I made a quick mental review of my past life and wondered who could have murdered Hector Slaight. I decided that a calm approach would be best and invited Detective Colson in. Under his arm he had a brown paper bag, which I at first assumed to contain a Persian melon. Shortly thereafter I knew that it was definitely *not* a melon, and I had not the slightest desire to examine either its texture or its appearance.

He stood in front of the fire, warming and wringing his hands. A very nice young man, I thought, well-mannered and obviously reluctant to accuse the Duchess and her progeny of murder.

178

Finally he gathered his courage together and turned to Her Serene Grace:

"Did you know the old Doc?"

"Very well. We miss him dreadfully."

"What was he like?"

"I loved him dearly."

"I mean, what kind of person was he? I know he died some time ago but I'd like to get a good picture of him in my mind."

The Duchess hesitated. How describe the old Doc? A thousand anecdotes concerning that fiddle-playing extrovert must have flashed through her mind.

"A delightful person. Perhaps a little eccentric."

"Capable of murder?"

(Personally I could think of a few he might have wanted to liquidate but they were all, unfortunately, still alive.)

The Duchess looked the detective straight in the eye. He turned scarlet.

"Most certainly not. What *is* all this about?"

"Do you know the people who have bought his house?"

"Slightly."

"Well, they needed some plumbing fixed in the cellar. When the men started digging they hit a bone. Thought it was an old leg of lamb the dog had buried and tossed it aside. Then they dug up the ribs and pelvis."

"So?"

"So they came down to the station and got us. The new owners co-operated very kindly so we didn't have to get a warrant. Our men found the rest of the skeleton."

I had a hysterical compulsion to laugh. So *that* was what was in the bag! Just the right size, just the right shape. I envisioned the Duchess playing Hamlet in the best Hampden tradition, standing on the hearth, turning the skull, and declaiming, "Alas, poor Hector! I knew him well."

My flight of fancy was interrupted. Colson's problem wasn't did we murder Hector. His headache was that he didn't know

179

who *had* been murdered and he hoped to heaven that we did.

My hands were clammy. He explained farther.

"There were no marks of violence on the skull." (I eyed the bag.) "The bones were in perfect state of preservation. This was a young man, we think, in excellent health."

"Were there any fillings in the teeth?" the Duchess asked it quietly. (Now surely he would hand us the contents of the bag!)

"No, they were in beautiful shape."

I don't know anyone who has no fillings. As to who it could have been I had not the foggiest notion. Besides, none of my intimate acquaintances was missing. I reluctantly admitted to complete bewilderment. So did the Duchess.

"Well, then," said Colson, "think hard, will you please? Is there anyone that disappeared? Some mistake the old doctor might have tried to cover?"

The Doc didn't make that kind of mistake, although once he did write on a death certificate: "Officiating Clergyman, Angina Pectoris. Cause of death, Rev. Thomas Travis," which considering the theological leanings of the deceased, may have had some truth in it!

No, there was little likelihood of this being a slip-up.

Undoubtedly everyone does make mistakes, and equally undoubtedly there are a lot of people who "never would be missed," but sitting on a scarlet sofa in a Chippendale parlor with a skull in a paper bag next to you is a situation in which, if you have any sensitivity at all, you do not quote even Messrs. Gilbert and Sullivan's better wisecracks.

I wanted a cigarette desperately, but years of training made me push the package deeper in my pocket. I was unsure of my protocol. Surely one does not smoke in the room with death, but just how much of a skeleton is essential for such consideration?

I came to the conclusion that the skull was the essential ingredient, and suffered in silence. So thin is our veneer of

180

civilization that every time I looked at that bag I could feel my hackles rise.

Tea was served.

I wasn't very hungry!

Detective Colson sat with a cup in one hand and an anchovy sandwich in the other. I recalled a young reporter who impressed me once with his worldliness by stating that he kept his sandwiches on the ice in the morgue.

Detective Colson had apparently become a permanent fixture at Tongueslip. I wished he would get out and take his paper bag with him.

Eventually he did.

Probably it was a melon in the bag. Anyhow, the skeleton was sent from expert to expert and the conclusion reached that it was an articulated study specimen brought in from abroad. The old doctor couldn't fix one for himself, because in New Jersey's archaic law no cadaver can be so cavalierly treated. That may be why we have no medical school in the state. It may not have been very wise to dispose of the skeleton under the cellar floor, but it would, we are inclined to think, have caused even more confusion had he deposited it in the rubbish barrel which stands at the curb!

I suppose that the bones of " X " were properly and respectfully interred in the potter's field by order of the medical examiner.

One thing I am sure of — the old Doc worked too long and too hard bringing people into the world and keeping them there ever to have assisted anyone out of it.

IT WAS only yesterday that I stood by the window at Tongueslip and looked through the lens in the plate-glass window which had been made by some errant BB in the hands of a small boy. Mary Katharine snuggled against my shoulder, and I put my nose against her, savoring the delicious smell of oil, powder, sun-dried linens, and warm fresh milk which, anywhere in the world, proclaims the presence of a baby.

The old doctor was leaving his home for the last time and I could not attend the services. Mary K. was only five days old.

It was, I think, at that moment that I first realized the kindness of nature which provides that the young can never feel for the aged the passionate love that the aged feel for the young. If they could, life and its inevitable ending would be too much to bear.

As it is, we sense a loss, feel regret, hope for another meeting, and adjust ourselves to the inescapable as time rolls on with increasing rapidity.

Suddenly the baby we held in our arms is reaching up to give us a bear hug before setting off to school, and another era is at an end.

At first there is a sense of emancipation unmixed with regret.

This new-found freedom manifested itself in my case by a lingering over breakfast, still in a wrapper; completely neglecting the beds; and drinking altogether too much tea. It is a period to which most young mothers look forward with breathless anticipation, and when they have arrived at it, they have not the remotest idea what to do with themselves!

This happy state of relaxation and ennui lasts until the

first meeting of the nominating committee of the church, the P.T.A., and other equally valuable institutions. Someone inevitably points the finger at another woman with time on her hands.

Immediately all pleasant sense of relaxation departs, and the rat race begins again. Worthy causes are legion, and if by chance one's name begins with "A" one is at the top of the list and must cope with the persuasiveness of the nominators which is reinforced by a fresh start after a good night's sleep. One succumbs. One never learns to say a firm "NO!"

Perhaps the increasing size of families among the college graduates is a manifestation of the evolution of a new technique in self-preservation. Well-distributed babies are excellent insurance against the danger of becoming a pathological chairman!

Still, committees are a necessity, but one wonders sometimes if there is enough woman power in the world to keep them all rolling. Perhaps it is fortunate that they come along when the hands are empty, and the void of inactivity keenly felt.

Once the children are in school, life is never quite the same again. New influences, some constitutional and some exceedingly subversive, creep into the microcosm known as home. No longer are Dad and Mother the final arbiters of propriety and wisdom: "My teacher says!" Mom and Dad are back numbers!

Our birding, for instance, had always been done most unscientifically. Odd marginalia recorded the finding of rarities and if, on occasion, the learned societies wished to know whether our find had a bill beset by six basal bristles or seven, we neither knew nor cared. Their acceptance or rejection of our treasure left us unperturbed.

Tommy was better educated. His teacher said — and so at the age of nine he started a meticulously recorded life list, and a daily log in which he recorded barometric pressure, temperature, wind direction, and other miscellaneous data.

Robert and I, of course, think birding should be fun, but to Tommy the life of an ornithologist was real and earnest.

His annual bird list followed a ritual that, to the uninitiated, is as incomprehensible as a lama's prayer wheel. It was compiled with a systematic intensity that defied wind, rain, snow, and heat, and the fact that the woodcock hunting season was on made no difference in the necessity to find a jacksnipe in the first week of November.

So far as I can piece the story together from what I heard and what I saw and participated in myself, Tommy selected Election Day to go to the Great Swamp.

He came to the old sawmill, with its slowly revolving water wheel, and watched for a while as the sawyer signaled the dog setters on the carriage, and directed their skillful turning of the great logs and the final meeting of tree and whining saw blade.

Then he wandered down the old road to the meadow, raced across the soft green turf in pursuit of a belated butterfly, and threw himself, hot and panting, on the old lichen-covered boulder beside the spring. The cold water looked inviting and he stuck his head into the pool, then shook it like a puppy until his unruly hair stuck out in even more directions than usual.

A man with a gun, intent upon the dog in front of him, passed the boy unseeing.

A whirr of wings was followed by the slam of both barrels and the cock pheasant dropped. Tommy froze, motionless. Didn't this guy know that a pheasant taken in woodcock season could cost him a hundred bucks?

Apparently he did, for when the dog retrieved the bird the gunner patted him quickly, took the game, and, lifting a nearby hummock, scooped out a bit of earth, wrapped the cock pheasant in leaves, replaced the tussock of grass,

184

and marked the spot with one of America's ubiquitous beer cans.

This accomplished, he again followed the dog. Tom climbed a nearby tree to watch proceedings. He had scarcely settled himself in the wide crotch when the gun blazed again. This time, through carefully focused glasses, Tom saw that the gunner had taken a hen pheasant.

A slow red anger started at his toes as he watched two pin-tailed ducks follow the pheasants into carefully scooped out holes, and a fierce resentment burned behind the blue eyes which followed the hunter's progress.

When the man disappeared from sight, Tom got his temper under control and came down out of the tree.

"Three days for woodcock, that crumb is going to beat the others to it and get his pheasants early. He'll come back when the pheasant season opens and pick them up."

A sudden harebrained thought darted between Tom's ears. It was not far to those first two beer can markers. If it weren't for the hen maybe he wouldn't — but hen pheasants were illegal game all the time, and they meant more birds next year.

Stealthily he edged through the bushes at the border of the meadow and then sauntered carelessly across the open field. He snatched the cock from its resting place and stuck it in the front of his shirt. But the bird was big and the long tail feathers curled up through his collar and stuck up behind his ears. He took off his shirt and wrapped the cock in it. Then he got the hen. The pintails joined the others and the shirt was heavy. He had to set the bundle down quite often as he made his way through the brush, and he checked it carefully to see that no blood was soaking through to give him away.

He realized that he should not take the road past the sawmill, so he struck across the marsh to the cat walk under the power lines. His sneakers squished in the mud and he

185

thought he heard someone behind him. He tried to run, but fell flat on his face in the ooze. By devious routes, known only to small naturalists, he finally made the security of home and, trembling with fear as much as with exhaustion, flung the shirt on the kitchen table and himself into Chloe's arms.

"What is it? Don't cry so, boy!"

"He shot the hen, he shot the hen!"

No word of all the legal technicalities poured out, only over and over: "He shot the hen, and I was afraid after I'd done it he might shoot me."

Finally Chloe managed to quiet him and washed his mud- and tear-streaked face. He sat at the long board table, tucking in waffles, while Chloe patiently plucked the birds.

Robert came in to get a drink of water and saw the feathers.

"What's this?"

Tommy told him.

Robert rubbed his ear with his fist and it made a small slapping sound, but it gave him time to think. He looked down from his great height at the little boy.

"That wasn't very smart, Tom, to monkey with that kind of man when he is carrying a gun. I can see why you did it, but we don't eat pheasant out of season either."

Chloe took the birds and hung them in the larder.

When I came in, she told me what happened. I must admit that I thought it was a job well-done, though I'd never have had the nerve to do it myself.

"Well, Mr. Arny didn't like it one little bit. He said we eat no pheasants out of season."

"Chloe, those birds are meat, and I've hardly had a decent chew of protein since Pearl Harbor. Meat just doesn't taste like it used to. This is Tuesday and the season opens in a couple of days."

"Miss Mary, careful where you tread!"

186

On Saturday the family sat down to dinner. Bob picked up the carving knife, sliced into the largest bird.

"What have we here?"

"An old Chinese delicacy," I said between my teeth.

Tommy looked bewildered. Robert smiled at him. "Your mother has just finished rereading *The Good Earth*, and she holds, with Wang Lung's wife, that meat is meat."

When we had said grace, the Duchess picked a bird shot out of her pheasant and laid it on the edge of her butter plate with a small, clinking noise. Through the absolute silence I observed that the pheasant season opened today.

After dinner Robert and I went out into the garden to have a cigarette and to look at the stars. It was a northern lights night, and we watched the tenuous fingers of the aurora reach and recede across the sky.

Finally Robert said very quietly, "Why did you put me on the spot like that?"

Still torn between conscience and fury, I tried to answer reasonably, "It wasn't very nice of me I suppose."

"Look, Sugar, I know that you think waste is wicked. I think it is even worse to flout the law. If the kids see us do it, what can we expect from them?"

"But *we* didn't break the law — it was the gunner."

"We profited by it."

"Well, then, it was bad judgment on my part. But I don't think a combination like that would happen again in a lifetime."

"See that it doesn't." He kissed me very gently.

I still don't know who was right about those pheasants, and I can't help wondering if most of the things that people quarrel over aren't like that. There are few times when a thing is dead right, or dead wrong. How simple life would be if they were, and how terribly dull!

Ethical problems like the eating of the pheasants came thick and fast in those first days of schooling. There must

187

be some proper answer to the statement, "All the other kids are allowed to," but so far we have not discovered it. The theory is, of course, that one brings up a child in the way that he should go, but the question is, What is the way? With three generations expressing their opinion in the matter, one finds oneself looking for a set of permanent values, and faced with the necessity of adapting to a rapidly shifting code of *lex* and mores.

There are, it seems to us, certain aspects of past tradition worthy of respect. Certainly it is strange that the present passionate pursuit of self-expression and individuality in education is producing regimented civilizations, whereas education in its formal origins produced the great leaders of democracy. There are other aspects too of twentieth century custom that leave room for improvement.

Our dearly beloved sister-in-law Martha Ann says I am Victorian. Her opinion is not shared, I fear, by most of my intimate acquaintances. Rather, I think, they expect a puff of smoke, slightly sulphurous, and a loud explosion, when I put in my appearance. Be that as it may, I resisted television.

It might be noted for the record that the Duchess resisted it too. My objection was that it was a waster of time which dwarfed even committee meetings; hers, that in Tongueslip it would be anachronism.

Robert, however, was determined that we should have a TV set. It was, he averred, unfair to our next door neighbors, the Loves, for us not to have one, since our children no longer lived at home but merely passed through it, snatching sandwiches and Cokes between rounds of what Johnny Love called " horsey gunnies " and space transistors.

This argument bore considerable weight with me because I am already eternally in Cynthia Love's debt. I used to write slick facile stories of café society. For years Cynthia read, criticized, and corrected them and editors rejected them. Finally, in complete exasperation, Cynthia told me the truth.

"They're awful. For heaven's sake, why don't you write about birds and animals and children, where you know what you're talking about?"

There are few surer tests of devotion than to read an unpublished manuscript and frankly state that it stinks.

Yes, if a TV set should be purchased out of decent consideration for Cynthia, that was definitely a point. Still I hesitated.

Robert was determined. He conceded the anachronism, and had a pine cabinet made for the set which melts with a minimum of clashing into the old leather books in the corner by the fireplace. But TV is still indisputably a product of the atomic age. He put the antennae in the attic, where it is inconspicuous among the stuffed tarpon, tanned snakeskins, and miles of electric train track.

The Duchess and I set our lips grimly, and with a proper air of martyrdom allowed that Robert certainly had a right to do as he pleased in his own house, particularly since the heat, light, food, clothing, and other needs of the flesh that are used therein derive chiefly from "The World's Best Tubemakers."

We, however, retained our inalienable right not to look at the thing, and retired to the middle room, ostentatiously carrying books, preferably nonfiction and very thick. It was pleasant to have the Duchess on my side for once. She usually allies herself with Robert or maintains a strict neutrality.

Three regularly constituted meals a day again became a possibility, and in fact there was a remarkable decrease in dawdling over them when an ironclad rule that no one could watch TV until all were finished eating was passed. These blessings were somewhat mixed when we found that most of the meal was taken up in bitter argument as to what program should be tuned in.

We endured that as long as we could, and I for one was ready to remove "The World's Best Tube" from the thing and settle the argument once and for all when fate took a hand. The Honorable Estes Kefauver appeared upon the scene.

Understand it was purely a sense of civic duty, a matter of political responsibility, that induced me to watch the hearings at all. In about half an hour I tore my attention from the screen long enough to discover the Duchess sitting beside me, and leaning forward intently.

Three regular meals were again a thing of the past. The Duchess and I sat with trays on our knees watching Senator Tobey flay his victims. The beds remained unmade, the dishes unwashed, the children sat in sullen fury, frustrated by the absence of Captain Video, and shushed and hushed beyond all reason.

Chloe sat and watched with us. There was no apple pie on Wednesday night.

Robert said nothing, but I detected just the slightest gleam of amusement in his eyes.

The Kefauver inquiry ended, and life returned to normal, but not the Pine Room. Our beautiful colonial library is now the gathering place of the clans. I adore Captain Video, that new Saint George, who fills the spot of longing inherent in all men for someone who will ride against the dragons, or the spacemen of evil, on a white horse, or in spaceships at high linn. Oh, lovely legend, and how full of meaning! Science, you have not changed man one whit!

"Mama" is an intimate friend of ours, we laugh uproariously at "Our Miss Brooks" and at George and Gracie, and we love Mr. Peepers, who fills another long-felt gap in the mores of our era; we live and learn with "Hall of Fame."

We move in another world now — a world where time and space are obliterated. The Grand National Horse Show, filled with so many sparkling memories for the Duchess, comes to her, since she can no longer go to it. We have ringside seats at conventions, and I do believe that the

190

knowledge that the people are watching reduces political chicanery to a minimum. I shall be *very* careful hereafter how I trim down blown up photographs.

Through this miraculous medium, far more potent than Aladdin's lamp, in that it brings knowledge and ideas, rather than gold and diamonds, into our possession — through this miraculous medium, I believe that we are nearer to government by the people than we have ever been before.

We have heard Mr. Romulo, and Mr. Dulles, and Mr. Malik with our own ears, and we are in a position to draw our own conclusions from the facts, not from someone's interpretation of them. Man need no longer be the victim of false news and sniping propaganda.

Yes indeed, television is a wonderful thing. It is a miracle. It is a great educational instrument. We at Tongueslip hope that one day Congress will go on the air.

Of course we have television! All of us at Tongueslip use it and enjoy it. We always wanted it and were delighted when Robert brought it home. Winter afternoons from four to six are a pleasure now instead of a holocaust. Peace reigns. I can digest my dinner.

No, definitely not, Robert. I will have no part in a personal airplane. I hate the things. They are a product of the hectic hemicycle, and besides, in the stable, which is the only place we could keep it, it would be a dreadful anachronism.

ANOTHER and more practical reason for not keeping a plane in the stable is that Hector Slaight would constantly pepper it with buckshot.

191

I remember one December evening when the blurping bang of a scatter-gun blasted the silence at exactly nine forty-seven. Being an avid "who-dun-it" fan, I notice time like that and make mental notes of dates. Maybe someday Detective Colson will come around with another set of questions. That time we'll be ready for him. In any case I find a nice wholesome murder a welcome relief from the literature of the pathological disintegration of the human soul.

This particular blurp, however, was followed by nothing more startling than utter silence at first. In a couple of days it was followed by something more tangible. Rats!

Rats sat on our bird feeders, rats scuttled along the beams of the goosehouse. Rats quarreled and squalled between the walls of Tongueslip itself. We knew with dreadful certainty what had happened. The Codfish — a name coined by Mary Katharine for Mr. Slaight — had at last hit Aluco the barn owl.

Robert went up to the hayloft, but Aluco was not there. All that could be seen was a pile of pellets, which in the interest of science was sent to Cornell University for study. The report we received back showed that our monkey-faced friend had, since the loft was cleaned in June, made way with seventy-four house rats, more mice than could be counted, and sixteen shrews. No bird bones were found in the debris.

Polly was for action. " Darn old Codfish. Hurting Aluco. Now look at the rats. His cats will eat them, huh? Well, why don't they? I'm going to kill the Codfish with a pitchfork. I'm going to eat him for supper."

" She loves her fellow men, preferably with parsley and egg sauce," said Tom.

The rest of us shared Polly's desire in silence and felt it a consummation " devoutly to be wished."

During the era of mourning for Aluco, Uncle Jim, Dad's and Aunt Mary's brother, came to call. We always looked forward to his visits, for we were sure to hear some fabulous yarn told in his inimitable and sometimes incomprehensible Lancashire dialect. We were not disappointed, Uncle Jim had a pip! He worked with the Mosquito Commission and had just come in from inspecting the drainage ditches in the meadows. There, he vowed, he had seen a *black* rat on the ice.

Everybody knows we don't have black rats on the meadows. They are the Asiatic carriers of bubonic plague, the villains in the history of the Black Death which changed all European history. Every ship that comes into harbor is quarantined against these bearers of disaster. Huge, circular rat guards are slipped onto the hawsers. Hydrocyanic acid gas is pumped into the holds. If plague rats ever got loose in New York City, the results would make an H-bomb look like a strawberry festival. We Americans have no immunity against plague. There is not enough vaccine on earth to inoculate New York City. Uncle Jim made a mighty story of it, and it was the more gripping because we knew that what he said about plague was true. We were equally certain that what he said he had seen was not.

When Uncle Jim had finished his yarn, he tapped out his pipe against his heel, spat accurately into the fireplace, and swilled six cups of tea in rapid succession. Then, hitching his trousers, which like Dad's always seemed to be in imminent danger of sliding over his hips, he allowed as how he'd better get along back to the laboratory men and set them to work to catch Monsieur the Ratto.

Meanwhile we watched the brown rats drag their long and revolting tails across the snow. We set snap rats at strategic places, and wished that the Codfish were locally engaged in the cheese business so that he would get his just deserts. But life isn't that way.

The wind shifted from the northwest and the weather abated. The ice melted, and the streams poured into the meadows, flooding them and forcing the wild creatures to higher land. With the southeast wind came the smell of burning oil, and the smog of black smoke which we can depend upon from that quarter. But it was heavier than usual, and with it was the odor of salt marsh.

Robert sniffed the breeze and rubbed the back of his neck with his pipestem. "That's odd, burning the meadows over at this time of year! Do you suppose that Uncle Jim wasn't drawing the long bow after all?"

He stood jingling the change in his pocket, watching the wild goose on the weather vane flying east. Then, with an easy swing, he was up in the pine tree, clambering its ladder-like branches clear to the top. From there he could see over the Codfish's garage, across the towns to the meandering Passaic, over the salt marshes to the Hackensack, and to the Palisades beyond. The Empire State and the Chrysler Buildings were lost in a haze of black smoke.

"I can't see any rats, but there's smoke all right. Systematic smoke from the Skyway to S-3."

We stood there wondering, and Tommy, a small edition of Dad in stance and speech, rubbed the back of *his* neck. He spoke slowly. "I don't think we should talk about this outside the family, but we've got to find Aluco. She's maybe hunting there and she'll get scorched."

"Why shouldn't we tell?" Polly piped.

"Look, Polly, if you tell, it will scare people."

Mary Katharine looked seriously at her father. "Daddy, you should tell Mr. Slaight. He deserves to be scared. If he hadn't shot Aluco we shouldn't have rats."

"Darling," I assured her, "one owl couldn't hold the breach against all the rats. You can't scare the Mr. Slaights of the world. They are so sure that they know better than God what is needed to keep nature in balance. You would have to go about shouting from the housetops, and even then they would not hear you."

194

"Well," Tommy insisted, "that comes under family solidarity, parsonage confidence, just as much as anything else does. We shouldn't tell. That is Uncle Jim's story, and you're always saying that we don't steal people's money and pass it around when they trust us, so we mustn't steal their story either."

The meadows burned for days, but we seemed to have the rat situation under control. No more holes were gnawed in the grain boxes. No more rats scurried as we went into the barn.

Polly, the persistent, said very little, but I missed her frequently, and finally I asked her where she was disappearing to. " The hayloft. I saw Aluco, but she's dragging a wing and I didn't want you all to go up and scare her. Here — " her grubby small hand stretched out and in it was a pile of pellets, knots of fur and bones which Aluco had spat out. " I'm going to send them in." She did.

The reply when it came was addressed to me.

" *Dear Mrs. Arny:*

From the handwriting on the package, we suspect that one of your children sent along the owl pellets. We are sorry that some of your collection has obviously been disturbed. We find in our examination the skulls and tarsi of four black rats. Since the damage has already been done, will you be good enough to send us the proper labels and dates and, as nearly as possible, the location in the Orient from which these pellets came? They are of particular interest in that there are remains of other small mammals indigenous to our area, and we cannot explain this mixture of species.

  " *Sincerely yours,*

       " *Curator of Mammals.*"

Someday, perhaps, I shall take that letter to Mr. Slaight. Meanwhile we have closed Aluco's old entrance and made her a better one on the east, where she can hunt toward the meadows immune from bird shot.

But I suppose that even the scientific evidence of the letter would not do any good. Nor would it avail anything to shout from all the housetops, "Aluco the barn owl, Buteo the hawk, Aquila the eagle preserve you from evil. They kill your enemies, the bearers of disease. They preserve your crops and your warehouses from destruction." The Slaights of the world could not hear.

We can only hope that Providence, like ourselves, has confidence in the men in the laboratories, and that the Coast Guard has been told that the next time a ship from Calcutta breaks upon the shore, not only the harbor master, but also the Public Health Service, should be notified.

Perhaps you will understand now why Tommy likes owls.

Since he has educated us in the matter very thoroughly, all of us at Tongueslip respect and admire owls. In fact, we are the defenders and champions of owls.

Mary Katharine and Polly, having heard the tale of the man who shot a doe that stood between him and her fawn, and of the plume seekers who murdered the warden in Florida, cannot see just why gunners call owls vermin. If taking a few pheasants or a duck for food makes a creature "vermin," then there are a lot of specimens in this category walking behind dogs in the field.

Hunters should be very carefully distinguished from gunners. They belong to a different breed. They do not require of a farmer that he label his cattle "COW" in large red letters, for the simple reason that they do not blaze away indiscriminately at everything that moves.

Sister Sally's husband, Doc, like Dad and Uncle Jim, is a hunter. I am devoted to Doc and his kind, who walk the fields of other men remembering that they are guests, who bring us news of fox and coon and rare birds, and who build nesting boxes and plant cover for game. These men conserve our resources instead of plundering them. Hunters are of paramount value to naturalists; gunners are anathema, an

196

incarnation of the devil, and as assiduously to be avoided. To encounter Satan with a loaded gun is to court disaster.

Anyone who does not believe in the devil is commended to a study of the telephone, one of his most successful inventions.

An excellent case could be made for this statement. For instance, how many quarrels have been started because those with red-hot tempers seized the little black talker before they cooled off? How many unnecessary committee meetings, how much gossip, how much slander can be traced directly to it? At Tongueslip the beastly thing rings incessantly. I should have taken it out long ago if it were not for one fact. I get the bird news fast over it. This compensates me for the, by count, seventy-three interruptions a day which it causes!

January 6 was off to a ripping start and I had not finished my breakfast tea when the phone screamed for attention. It was d'Arcy. " There is a snowy owl at the shore. Want to see it? " We did!

Tommy and Bob and I put on our ski suits, mittens, and heavy boots and gathered our binoculars and cameras. D'Arcy joined us. The forty miles to Jones Beach rolled by with never a bad moment. The rest of the civilized world were hugging their fireplaces, or — lacking these — their radiators. January 6 was cold.

We drove across the marshes, where the rime made silver patterns on the cattails, and saw a harrier beating its way upwind. The grasses on the dunes whipped in circles, drawing fairy rings on the sand. Myrtle warblers drifted from bayberry to bayberry with their golden rumps flashing in the sun. Jones Beach, and not a car in sight!

We parked along the roadway above the pavilion, for there was not any competition for space, and opened the door of the car. The wind caught it and tore it back on its hinges with a rending sound. Tommy stepped to the sand and rocked back on his feet. He shouted, but we could not hear him.

Robert took his hand and mine and motioned to the dunes. " Get to the leeward, we can't take this for long! " So we edged our way between the great mountains of sand toward the shore.

Along the beach the waves pawed at the land, great streaming manes of spume blowing back to sea from their crests. Each shell and pebble stood in a tiny pillar which the eroding wind had carved from the place below it. Sand blew into our faces and filtered through our nostrils into our mouths. We bent into the gale, Robert and I with linked arms, d'Arcy flanking us, and Tommy plowing along behind the slight windbreak which we made.

" He'll be on this side, out of the wind, under the ledge of the dunes," I screamed into Robert's ear. He nodded.

A white speck showed against the golden sand high to the left. " There he is. Take it easy." We crept forward, nearer and nearer. The bird turned his head, stretched his great white pinions, and was air-borne. With leisurely strokes he beat upwind, but his progress was slow and we could walk faster. The gale blew him toward us and he fought desperately. He began to labor and faltered. Each deep stroke seemed slower than the last, and finally, exhausted, he settled again.

We were close to him now. Perhaps a hundred feet. He stared at us. His great golden eyes slitted against the sand and the light. We waited for his huge head to turn and edged closer. I set up the camera and Bob held it against the wind. The range dial showed eighty feet as the lens swung into position. We moved forward — seventy feet, fifty, thirty. Still the unblinking eyes stared into ours. Now we could see the tawny crescents on his breast and the great talons, bigger than my hands, moving uneasily, clasping and unclasping.

Tommy was trembling so that he had to lean his binoculars on a fallen scrub oak. I lowered the tripod and inched forward again. Eighteen feet, fifteen. The great round head filled the camera field. There was no point in going nearer. " I could grab him." The words formed on Tom's lips soundlessly. "Go ahead," Bob signaled.

The small figure flattened against the sand and began to worm its way. Indian great-great-grandmother came into her own for those moments. The owl stared at the towering figures of two men and a woman. The boy moved carefully, taking advantage of every clump of grass, every hollow, every leaf, so that only the slowly narrowing gap between him and the majestic hunter from the arctic indicated that he was not fixed in time and space. Ten feet, five. Tom's hand began to stretch forward, tense, white-knuckled. The owl turned his head and the snow-white feathers ruffled in the gale. The boy's fingers opened and his hand was cupped. His wrist flicked like lightning and his palm was against the furry flanks. The bird rose in a majestic sweep and soared downwind. I turned to watch him, white, like a disembodied spirit against the cobalt winter sky. Borne by the gale that screamed across the island, he swept out of sight among the myrtle.

We bent over Tommy and set him on his feet. He grinned: "I touched him. But my fingers wouldn't close. They're cold!"

I put his stiff hand into the front of my jacket, right against the skin, the behavior of mothers from time immemorial, the gesture that shows how close, how very close, we are to our savage ancestors. We huddled under the dune and let the sun beat down upon us. We swallowed hot soup from our thermos and talked excitedly about the owl.

"By golly he was big," Tommy chortled. "Couldn't have hung onto him if I'd got him. He must be three feet high."

If you were a boy on your tummy in the sand, you'd think he *was* three feet high. It's really a little more than two. But I would give more than I care to say to have felt against my hand the warm, white, wondrous feathers of Nyctea, the great snowy owl, ghost of the tundra, phantom of the North.

[25]

PERHAPS it was because of Dell Buttrey's interest in our owl adventure that we liked him so thoroughly, but I think it went deeper than that. As the new clergyman, stepping into Dad's pulpit, he never did what so many men would have done. He never tried to make either us or the parish feel we were back numbers, and that he was the cock of the walk. He grasped the difficulty of our position and made it easy for us by always including us.

One of the many gracious things he did was to ask favors of us, and there was one that he asked for which we shall always be grateful.

He came in one rainy Friday night and sat down wearily. We recognized the symptoms at once. There was an insoluble problem.

"Folks," he began, "the *General Sturgis* docks at dawn tomorrow. There has been a mistake. Somebody counted wrong and there is an extra Displaced Person aboard. I don't know a thing about him except that he doesn't speak a word of English. Will you take him in?"

Robert started to speak.

"Just a minute, Bob, before you answer. I must in fairness tell you that you have to guarantee that he will have employment, that he will not become a public charge, and that you will be responsible for him. It's a lot to do for a pig in a poke."

Robert thought a minute. "What else can you do? You can't send the poor devil back. Of course we'll take him."

Dell's shoulders straightened and he grinned. "O.K. Be at the dock at seven A.M., will you?" We nodded.

I admit it. When I got out of bed at five thirty the next morning I did so with a revolting smugness. Boy, were we virtuous! Bighearted! Honest to God Christians! I polished my halo with my sleeve and put it on at a becoming angle. Really, you know, I was the saint. Robert had to go to work. He wouldn't even do the meeting.

I dressed the three children, who were so sleepy that their ordinary adaptability would not function; filled them with fried eggs and bacon, much of which was left on the plates; and set off for New York.

The drive across the meadows in the early morning is in itself an adventure. You pass through the sleeping cities, silent under the pearl-gray dawn. The rising sun catches the towers of New York and makes them gleam like the minarets of Baghdad. The mist rises from the salt marshes and a wintering flock of red-winged blackbirds wheels up from the flats. Gulls whiten the drive-in theater, now abandoned.

The turn as you go down into the Lincoln Tunnel is one of the most wonderful sights on earth. The harbor filled with great ships, some floating high, some laden down to the Plimsoll line, stretches before you, and a tiny figure, far to the south, reaches into the sky, holding her torch aloft for all the world to see.

Then down you go through the glorified tile bathroom that is the tunnel itself, and up again into the slowly stirring streets, where rock doves plod leisurely down Broadway and here and there a pushcart vendor is setting out his wares.

As you come to the docks, all manner of odors assail your nostrils: coffee, spices, fish and clams; the ether smell of rotting oranges and the crisp, clean odor of celery. You park under the West Side Highway and go into the dark, damp pier.

It's hotter than the hinges on that pier in August, but in February it is perishing cold. The wind lashes across it till your eyes cry and your fingers ache. You can go into the waiting room if you want to, but it is hot and stuffy and smells of the city, unwashed humanity, and stale cigars, an odor overlaid always by the stench of untrained cats.

We stood on the pier until we froze, thawed in the waiting room, and went back to the pier. The *Sturgis* was still at quarantine. There were hours of waiting. Finally she nosed into dock, and there was a clattering of winches, a splashing of ropes, and the shouting of men, while from the decks came a deep sigh, almost a moan, from the group who had come at last to America, the promised land.

The cargo was unloaded first. Nets swung over the gap between ship and dock, crates, boxes, machinery, goods, and then a few people trickled down the gangplank.

First off were the women with children. We had expected to see a motley crew, tattered and battered by the tides of war. It took us quite a while to connect the tags which they all had, "Church World Service," with the neat American clothes they wore. But there were things revealing and heart-rending.

I have very adequate French, and a little German, composed largely of such jawbreakers as "*die Schwefelsäure,*" which means sulphuric acid; "*uringeboren,*" which speaks for itself; and other equally useful conversational gambits.

Because of their very starkness the exchanges at the barrier were comprehensible.

"My brother . . . after all these years."

Eyes filled with tears. "Not Lubin Castle, Dachau."

"Only I am left."

"Your mother . . . Siberia."

"My other sons . . . before Moscow."

Everywhere, everywhere, everywhere, the news of death and destruction! Yet everywhere a look of hope. The men reached eagerly for the cigarettes shoved at them through the green picket barrier, and they smoked them down till they burned their fingers. Then from their lapels came the pin kept for such occasions, and the butt was fastened to the pin and smoked down to the last puff.

Chocolate bars, handed through to the children, were turned

202

over and over and nibbled and put into pockets to be stored against a more desperate hunger. Hot coffee, handed to mothers, was given to the babies. Habit . . . habit . . . habit.

My damnable smugness dropped into the Hudson River with a splash which left salt spray on my face. If I were a sentimental person, one might have thought it was tears.

Hour after hour we waited. All the passengers were gone. And then a lone figure, carrying a suitcase that shone with newness, strode down the pier. The immigration officer looked at his papers and yelled. "Hey, Charlie! This one ain't got a sponsor. What'll I do?"

"Poor guy, that's tough! Send him back."

The children and I waved violently. "Officer, officer, here we are!" The blue-coated figure came toward us, took our papers, and returned to his companion.

We held our breath. We waited. We saw the rubber stamp — oh, blessed, blessed rubber stamp! — and heard in the silence of the deserted pier a small smack.

The man came toward us, through the gate, set down his suitcase, took off his hat, clicked his heels, and bowed.

"*Gnädige Frau,*" was all he said.

All the way home from New York something fought inside me. Why was I doing this anyhow? Here was a German, the kind of guy who had killed my friends and pillaged all Europe. Why didn't I chuck him into the salt marsh?

I'm glad I didn't decide that that was what I should do. It is a help to know that, even if he had been a Nazi, my upbringing would have prevented it.

It is seemly that at one time or another in life situations should arise that are previews of crises. To know in advance how you are apt to behave when the chips are down is helpful.

Of course one never really does *know,* but experience has taught us that in moments of real stress one is apt to follow the pattern of the little habits of a lifetime. Many of these are inherited, and it is understood that if the devil himself were to call at Tongueslip, he would be treated courteously, for, after all, he would be a guest and he has certain admirable qualities. Chief among these is persistence.

So I did not chuck our D.P. into the salt marsh. Before we got home I was very glad that I hadn't, for on a long and lonely stretch by the Hackensack River the car swerved horribly, as though, having sensed my mood, it had decided to settle for no halfway measure and was determined to fling us all into the black sucking mud of the swamp. It almost turned turtle.

We had a blowout. I sat there, holding onto the wheel and silently resenting the injustice of the situation. Our D.P., however, had been trained in German efficiency on captured American equipment. He held out his hand for the keys.

I gave them to him.

He got out of the car, clicked with mechanical precision to the trunk, laid the proper tools neatly on a piece of folded newspaper lest a speck of rust be formed, and changed the tire with a rapidity that I have never seen equaled. While he was kneeling there at the side of the road, a squadron of bombers on a practice run zoomed over and I watched them idly, till Mary Katharine said, " What's the matter with *him*? "

His face was as white as paper and he crouched against the side of the car, waiting for the roar of bombs that had become so inevitably associated in his mind with American B-24's.

Until that moment it had never really penetrated my consciousness that *our* planes could mean fear and death to anyone. Somehow when I thought of a bomber it always had a ig black swastika on it.

He brushed himself off, replaced the tools so that for the first time in history they did not clang every time we hit a bump, and we proceeded homeward.

At dinner that night we began what was to be a long and harrowing piecing together. Robert has a little Russian, gleaned from the days of visiting Soviet engineers, and this, together with my halting German, made communication possible if slow.

He was not a German at all. He was a Pole, a Protestant Pole, remnant of that sect so persecuted at the time of Luther, because it was easier to burn them at the stake than to refute their arguments.

I should have guessed from the way he looked at Tom, as though somehow he had found something again. I should have sensed it from the way he ate an apple and left neither seeds nor core. We understood the more obvious signs of course, the high cheekbones, the dreadful pallor, the way he ate very little and kept his hands close to his plate, protecting.

He had been a carpenter in Poland. The Germans came into the little village late at night and took them all to the compound. Then there was fighting and artillery and confusion, and the Russians came in. They asked everyone if he had friends in America. He noticed that those who did not have were put in a line and booted into order. What had he to lose? He had kin in America, so he claimed them. He did not go into the mines with the friendless, but into the army. He was captured by the Germans before Stalingrad and sent back to the Fatherland as a prisoner of war.

He was lucky there, for he was put out to labor on a farm where the people were as good to him as they dared be. At least he did not starve to death. He did not know what had become of his father, his mother, his brothers, his wife, and his child. He will never know. Most of all he longs for his little son, blond, blue-eyed, just like Tom.

At the end of the war he was liberated, and, being a good carpenter in a country that needed to be rebuilt, he found work. He saved. He took great care of all that he had, but he could not buy enough to eat or to wear. Church World Service had helped him, and here he was.

We taught him English. He taught us much more. Now he is a boss carpenter. We have just made out his income tax for him. It is substantial, and increased by interest on a bank account that surpasses ours. He has his first citizenship papers, but, best of all, there is light in his eyes again.

I think that the answer to why he is what he is lies in the kind of faith revealed by our conversation on that first night. "Please, I want right away to get insurance so that you will not have to take care of me if I am sick or have no work."

It seemed to me such a dreadful thing that he should fear or worry now. "Listen, friend," I said, "God has gotten you through war and prison and bombings and invasion, and even through the United States Customs. He certainly will not fail you now. Stop worrying. He will take care of you."

His shoulders straightened, and he clasped and unclasped his hands between the knees of his spotless shabby suit.

"*Gnädige Frau, Mein Herr, Grossmutter* . . . to me it seems that *Herr Gott* must become very weary of taking care of those who will not take care of themselves."

[26]

OUR D.P. worked in our garden, helping to repair the ravages of winter and to plant seeds for a new crop, and learning the English language.

Cold must have made a deep impress upon him, for instead of tossing the fallen limbs on the fire, he cut them into neat lengths and tied them in bundles of fagots.

Heat, however, affected him worse than cold. The sizzling days of early June left him, and us, wilted and exhausted.

Even under the new mulberry tree no breath of air was stirring. Mary K. and Tom decided that we should all go swimming. It was Polly, as usual, who thought we should take a picnic, and Polly who insisted that Daddy would rather be interrupted at the office than miss a swim at the lake. So it was arranged that we would take Robert's suit along with us and meet after our plunge, at the car.

The water was cool and clear and refreshing, and after an hour of luxuriating we came out on the beach thinking the world a lovely place and, laughing and chatting, walked along the line of cars to our own.

I put my hand on the door handle and the world took on a sudden stormy cast. Tied to the steering wheel was a ticket, a summons to appear in court on Friday, June 25, at nine thirty in the morning.

That it should be on that date was the crowning insult. I had plans for the twenty-fifth — it was our wedding anniversary — and I did not enjoy the prospect of spending the morning in court. I strolled down the line of cars to see who would be keeping me company, and noted with increasing interest that there was not another ticket in sight.

Sweet reason and meekness are qualities toward which I have ceased to strive. I made the effort once but it was fruitless, and when Tommy pointed out the fact that not only were we the only ones with a ticket, but we were also the only Essex County car, and Mary K. noted the large black Cadillac smack in front of a fire hydrant and unticketed, the minimal quantity of calm which I have wrested from life left me and I blew my top. Our D.P. was paralyzed. Such language to use about the police! Didn't I know that was dangerous? If I was heard I might disappear. I continued to exercise my right as an American to freedom of speech.

Robert and George strolled up at this strategic moment. Robert, as you know, is always collected, and George is a lawyer. They pointed out the uselessness of fury and recommended a further plunge in the lake, which suggestion only made me madder, but I followed it when we had discovered that the only "No Parking" sign was seventy-five feet from where our buggy stood, flat against a wall, and hidden by a doorway at that. All my rebel ancestors, Pilgrim, Huguenot, and Revolutionary, screamed for blood, and I knew that if I didn't calm down in the lake there would be an explosion of major proportions.

"I won't pay a fine for parking here if I go to jail for it," I frothed and yes, I admit it, I cussed. George and Bob tried their best to cool me off before I met a cop, but their reasonableness had the same effect that pouring gasoline on a fire has. When I am angry I want someone to be angry with me. What's the use of being sore when everybody treats you like a child in a tantrum?

On June 25 I dressed myself in my best bib and tucker, firmly resolved to act as well as look like a lady, and drove twenty miles to court. I parked the car in a pay lot for security reasons, and walked a dusty dripping half mile to the courthouse.

After some searching I located the clerk of the traffic court and, with what I thought was admirable restraint, handed him the ticket. He didn't even look up. "Where's the two bucks?" he demanded.

"There aren't going to be any two bucks."

"Huh?"

I repeated it with deadly courtesy. "There aren't going to be any two bucks. I'm not guilty."

"You'll have to tell it to the judge." (I had always thought that a cartoon line, but here it was in the flesh.)

"That's what I intend to do." My voice shook and he mistook it for weakness.

"Come back next week, same time, and tell your story."

Ah! blessed Robert, who insists that everything, even the small print, be read before you sign! I knew my ground.

"Beg pardon, but I was summoned to appear before this court at nine thirty A.M. on the twenty-fifth of June. I am here. I have fulfilled the terms of the summons. Where is the judge?"

208

The clerk shifted, he hemmed, he hawed, and finally he had to admit it: "Court is not in session."

What a stinker I am! I had him neatly and I loved it. He put out his hand for the ticket. "Here, I'll give you a postponement."

I grabbed that ticket as though it had been an elusive rabbit, and I smiled sweetly, though I expect to him it looked more like an exasperating grin. He opened his mouth and swallowed. I braced myself for a blast.

"Mrs. Arny, this is a funny thing for me to say. You've got us over a barrel. And why? Because most people would rather cough up two bucks than spend a half day getting justice. It's a lot of work to get justice. It takes time. And then they yell that the courts stink, and the cops stink, and you get justice for dough. You don't get justice for dough, Mrs. Arny. You get justice when you're ready to fight for it.

"Nobody ever fought for it in this court before, so we don't see much use in having the judge here day after day for nobody to come and plead to."

He got up from his desk, came around, and opened the door for me. "You take that ticket and you go home with it like a good girl. Then you stick it up in your mirror and you look at it once in a while. Then when somebody starts yelling, 'Dumb cop,' at you, you look at it real hard, and remember one dumb cop told you he wished more people would stand up for their rights instead of coughing up because they're lazy."

As I walked down the hall, I heard him muttering under his breath, "I'm not sure if it ain't as much perjury to sign the summons and send in the samoola when you ain't guilty, as . . ." The rest was lost in the scream of a siren and I didn't hear it, but I'll bet it was good.

I returned from court triumphant and unconquerable. The world was definitely my oyster, and when at our celebration the talk turned to birdbanding, as it often does, and comments were made about the attainments of certain individuals for whom I have no deep and abiding love, I thrust my neck out some six feet and averred that if you were going to band a bird you should go get it yourself.

An osprey, for instance, should provide some excitement. They usually nest about forty feet up in a dead tree. They have knocked a good many people out of trees and onto the rocks. They really presented a challenge.

Mary the Mighty flexed her chest belligerently. If our friends had been wiser, they would have assured me that they knew I could band a tiger and let it go at that. But they seemed dubious of my prowess, and the more dubious they were the more pigheaded my determination became.

I had said I would band an osprey and, though I very much wanted to back down, I couldn't. I couldn't even use the lame excuse that I could not find one. We spend our summers at Shelter Island.

Shelter Island lies between Montauk and Orient Point on Long Island, and the water there is so clean and clear that you can stand on your head in it and let it wash over your open eyes sweeping the cobwebs from your brain and the cares from your heart. To the naturalist it is a paradise, for it combines salt and fresh water, meadows and woodlands, tide flats and sandspits. Deer leap in the early morning mist-filled meadows, foxes walk quickly along the well-worn trails. Goldfinches swing on the wild blue chickory and the air is filled with the smell of green growing things.

To a birder the most fascinating thing is the osprey colony. Everybody knows it is there. There are about eighty pairs of these handsome eagles of the sea, and they soar across the waves on pinions as wide as a man can stretch, black and silver, catching the sparkle of the seashore sun.

Only the bald eagle, the peregrine falcon, and the goshawk can compete with the osprey in furious defense of their nests. Unfortunately I knew that and so did Robert.

What I should have done was egg him on to telling me I could *not* do it. But I was stubborn, and I think he felt that if ever anyone had asked for it I had. He steadfastly refused to give me an out.

We set about planning with care and deliberation, and were delighted when Mr. Tom Young, an old hand at climbing, who knows the island like the palm of his hand, said he would help us. He had a good nest lined up, one with the young nearly fledged, and he would take us to it.

The day came for the great adventure. The young birds were almost ready to fly, and if our intrusion frightened them from the nest, no serious harm would be done. We had watched young sea eagles learning to fly before, and knew the miracle that would take place before they were air-borne.

Often the eyrie is located on a small island where sustained horizontal flight is impossible. Sometimes it is on a channel marker, completely surrounded by swiftly moving water. The young birds begin by holding onto the edge of the nest and flapping their wings. Then they fly vertically and drop back into the nest. When the day comes for them to make their first sustained flight, the parents fly beside them, and if the young flag, they peel off like fighter planes and bear up their weary children upon their own sustaining wings.

It is a breath-taking and moving sight to behold, and each year I watch it with a sense of wonder and security and awe, for to me it is the present translated into the rolling phrases of the past, where Jehovah speaks: "Ye have seen what I did unto the Egyptians, and how I bare you on eagles' wings."

Yes, it was safe now for the ospreys, and armed with our bands, which bear our own number and direct the finder to notify the Fish and Wildlife Service, carrying cameras, and wearing gauntlet gloves, we set forth for the fray, mustering our courage as we went.

We arrived at the tree which Tom had chosen, and I started up the gnarled old trunk. The greatest hazard at the beginning was poison ivy. The tree was laden with it. As I climbed higher the branches began to crack ominously.

The parent birds came in screaming, with talons out for a strike. My hands, covered with huge gauntlets, began to sweat and slip. I was sorry I'd made an issue of ospreys! But I reached the edge of the nest. I could hear the camera grinding below.

The problem above *had* to be faced. An osprey nest weighs as much as a ton and is made of dead wood, seaweed, old fish nets, and anything else which looks interesting to a sea eagle. It overhangs, and you have to get over the ledge to reach the young. This accomplished, I found myself facing two young birds with blood-red eyes, erected crests, and talons working convulsively. A sharp breeze passed my head and I knew that Madam Osprey was on the job.

I reached in and took the near bird. The descent from the tree was complicated by the fact that one hand was occupied with a flapping sea eagle, and the other was shaking like a bowl of Jello in a high wind, but I reached the base intact.

There the band was affixed, the young osprey calmed with a nice bit of fish, and photos were taken. Then up I went to put him back. When I tried to reach the other bird, I couldn't. The nest is ten feet across and even by leaning over the edge and swimming in the air, I could not stretch the distance. I dared not get into the nest lest it collapse. Ospreys use the same nest for years and to destroy it would be a shame. I came down, and the men went up. This left me with the camera and I applied myself to it diligently.

It remains a profound conviction of mine that if you claim to have banded a bird, you should go and get it, not send someone else where you are afraid to venture. I had done so, and now I personally could relax. Tom Young and Robert had more sense than I had anyway and I was sure that they would handle the situation adroitly. They could get the other bird and I would photograph.

All was going well except that there was camera trouble. Something small and yellow kept appearing in the bottom corner of the finder. It must be on the ground glass because as I followed the men up the tree trunk the small and yellow kept pace. They reached the nest and the camera stopped moving. Madam Osprey came in diving, Bob put an arm to ward her off, and the small and yellow crept right into the nest. I stopped photographing.

Polly had followed the men up on the opposite side of the tree and found an outjetting branch where she chinned herself over and right into the eyrie! Down came the sea eagle screaming vituperations. Down went my heart to my heels! The baby could never survive a fall. I had reckoned without our Polly! She was between the two young ospreys and their mother couldn't hit her without hitting them.

Bob and Tom Young came down, one with a young osprey, one with a young Arny, and the adventure was completed.

We retired to the shelter of the woods and watched the nest for some time. The parent birds held a caucus, inspected the supports and structure of their home, dressed the feathers of their young, and, apparently quite satisfied, went off fishing. In a few minutes they returned, calm and serene, bearing the noonday meal.

Our serenity took longer to reassert itself. The quick banging of heart against ribs, the caught breath, the weakness of knee, remained for several hours. But by the time we had had a swim, watched the terns soar and dive, picked up an armful of conchs, and investigated the egg clutch of a black racer cunningly hidden in the sand, things had calmed down enough that we could wonder about our ospreys.

They will fly south each winter as far as Rio, and every year they will repair their nest against storm and hurricane before they go. Next spring they will beat their way north, come back to this same tree, lay their clutch of spotted eggs, and incubate them. Each time they leave the nest they will

213

cover the downy young with wet seaweed to shade them from the scorching sun. Each time they fish they will dive from tremendous height, rouse with a shaking of water droplets, and head for their home, carrying their catch head forward to cut the wind resistance.

How can they know their path through the trackless waste of ocean, fly without compass, know the date of their return, and find along the endless miles of shore this one tree in all the world, alight and call it home? Surely, surely this is not " blind chance "!

We know what they do from the bands we place upon their golden shanks. But we don't know how. The pedants call it migratory instinct, but we can think of a shorter and better word.

[27]

IN THE days of early autumn the osprey circled wider and wider on her flights. Her red eyes focused on a fragment of fisherman's net caught in the sand on a lonely beach. She spiraled down and with black and silver wings, stretched back to break her speed, came in for a landing.

Warily she eyed the knotted cords, then, deciding that they were not a trap for her, she seized the net with her curved beak and loosened it from the surrounding sand. A cork float attached to the edge offered a good purchase for her talons, and no threat of entanglement.

She moved her wings in majestic sweeps and carried her trophy to her eyrie. There she wove it into the supporting timbers of her nest, nudged at the massive structure, found it secure now against the gales of winter, and rested.

Then, driven by an urge that she could neither understand

nor resist, she towered into the blue September sky, and started her long drift south.

So through the days and nights of early autumn the great flocks move sunward. Migration, the miracle and the mystery, challenges all living things. It is a force more driving than any other, more inclusive, more perplexing.

Tommy believes, and we with him, that human beings have the instinct still. He is particularly aware of it since during each migratory period he, with his lares and penates, is forced to migrate to the third floor because of incursion on his nesting territory.

Human migration occurs predictably. In the fall of the year, just when the first wave of chickadees comes in from the north, we begin to get telephone calls: "May we drop in for the week end or for a night in the middle of the week?" It is a fixed feast.

We can sleep four extra at Tongueslip — at a serious pinch, six. But do our house guests arrive at socially spaced intervals? No, indeed. We said it before and we say it again, they come south with the chickadees and north with the robins.

I remember one such week in the fall of 1953. There was an ecclesiastical conference in town; Robert was the chairman of the pulpit committee for our church, and the first wave of the chickadees had swept into the apple tree at Tongueslip.

At eleven in the evening there was a cautious knock on the door. Brother Vin had caught a ride on a transport. Could we sleep him? We could. At seven A.M. the phone rang insistently. "There is a delegate for whom we have made no reservation. Can you take her?" We could gladly. At three o'clock friends from New England called: "We're on the way to Florida. Can we come to Tongueslip tomorrow?" Nothing and nobody we would rather see. "Please do come and please bring us ten quarts of milk and one quart of cream. There's a milk strike here."

We sent Tommy to open the blanket chest and drag out the

215

covers, which of course reeked of paradichlorobenzene. In the ordinary course of events this would have been a simple matter. The sun had shone unremittingly for ten weeks. No single drop of rain had fallen. The earth was powder-dry and the parched air would have absorbed anything. Robert was practicing the anthem for Sunday — " As Torrents in Summer." It did the trick. At the precise instant at which Tom finished hanging ten blankets on the clothesline the heavens opened and the rains descended. Could the water soak into the ground? By no possible means. It discovered the window well on the east of Tongueslip and filled the cellar to a depth of two inches before we discovered it.

Tommy rescued the blankets and we spread them all over the attic, hoping at least to diminish the odoriferous resemblance to a Pullman washroom.

We managed to get the beds made up, and to pluck marigolds and chrysanthemums in the downpour and place them at strategic points in each bedroom, as well as on the proper tables throughout the house. We bought a twenty-pound turkey and concomitants, and sat back peacefully relaxed and awaiting our guests with happy anticipation.

Five minutes of peace so filled me with boundless energy that I went to the kitchen to polish some silver, only to discover a sudden and dramatic lack of hot water. That our hot-water heater should have gone on the blink was of course not surprising, but when I called Public Service, I was informed that a man could not come until evening. I protested that I did not wish Mrs. John Olsen, of New Hampshire, to return to that spotless state under the impression that Montclair's church people belonged to the great unwashed. Mr. Public Service informed me that according to pleas so far received the entire United States of America was about to labor under the same misapprehension. The ladies who had the delegates from Utah, Seattle, Florida, Chicago, Cincinnati, Texas, and several points between, had the same tale of woe.

216

Nevertheless, though this was a Congregational affair, and water was not therefore of paramount importance, he would do his best. Water is of paramount importance to Congregationalists! We occasionally drink it!

Eventually Mr. Public Service arrived and hot water issued steaming from the pipes. I gathered myself together for a journey to Brookdale where I had a lecture to deliver. Frayed and jaded, I spoke at length of the calming beauties of nature, and prayed silently that I had encompassed every contingency so that I could get to the meetings downtown in time to encounter the clergy.

I encountered the gentlemen, hundreds and hundreds of the gentlemen, and tried to put the best foot I could forward, while examining what they put forward themselves in the light of the pastoral needs of our parish.

Breathless and puffing, I arrived at Tongueslip, to discover that in a moment of aberration I had forgotten that I was supposed to preside at a P.T.A. meeting that evening. Appropriately enough the title of the program was " What Is Your Headache? " My headache was that the projectionist was sick.

Nobody ever should tell me that the adolescents are a problem. Without Tommy and Pierre Adidge I should have been foundered. Those two young gentlemen gathered themselves together, took the films to school, and ran them.

As the subject was the problems of the teen-agers, and nobody in the audience was aware of who was in the projection booth, Tom and Pierre got an earful. On the way home they looked at each other and commented simultaneously, " So grownups think we're queer! "

" Can't you see why those kids did what they did, Mom? "

" It's simple, Mrs. Arny, it's because . . ."

Alas, I was too weary to listen. A great discovery in the sociological sciences is floating somewhere in mid-air between here and the George Innes Junior High School. Maybe a child psychologist would do well to show those films to adolescents.

217

Maybe it's like the army which underwent years of patient research to determine what climates and what soldiers should be put together. Finally somebody came up with the brilliant suggestion that each draftee be asked, "Which do you like best, hot weather or cold weather?"

I staggered wearily up two flights of stairs. Mary Katharine was sound asleep in Chloe's room, Polly on our couch. I staggered down.

Mrs. Olsen came in and joined the conversation around the fire and told us about her home in New England. You guessed it! The phone rang.

Cousin Bett was coming to New York in the morning. She certainly wanted to see us. Our invitation came from the heart. We adore Cousin Bett. The Duchess saw an opportunity for festival, so she phoned Cousin Edith in Bryn Mawr.

Cousin Edith could, I believe, enter the Grand Central Station, sit down at the information booth, start pouring tea, and create out of this great cross section of America a homogeneous and fascinating social occasion. She has a gift for making everybody feel that he is somebody. In moments of despondency it is to her that I turn, for somehow when she has listened to my platitudinous conversation for ten minutes, I feel that it would have made Shakespeare's dialogues feeble by comparison, that I am the best-dressed woman in America, and that my judgments and opinions are profound and world-shaking. I find myself sitting up straight, with my stocking seams parallel, and thinking, " By golly, I'm folks! "

In other words Cousin Edith is a highly desirable guest. The warmth of the invitation elicited response. Cousin Edith would come.

After Mrs. Olsen had departed for the morning meeting, I started shifting beds and bedrooms. This, of course, required sheets. Twelve beds take twenty-four sheets, no matter how you slice it, and with twelve sheets at the laundry the linen cupboard was bare. Nor could I borrow. Six hundred delegates were being slept in town, and I think that five hundred and ninety-nine of them were in beds belonging to our friends. Nobody had any linen, and nobody could wash any — it was still pouring!

Polly and I went downtown. There was not a parking place in sight. I went round and round and round the block. Cars from every state in the Union lined the curbs. The white slips in the windshields informed me that they belonged to "visitors to the Eastern Regional Conference." They weren't apt to move for several hours. I turned to Polly: "Darling, next time round I'm going to drop you off. Go into Hahne's. Get the man at the counter by the door to get Ella Bliss and tell her I need twelve percale single bed sheets and twelve pillow cases."

Polly did not look enthusiastic, but she went. My beloved Ella, who is the manager of said beautiful store, came through as she always does, and I had only to circle the block twice before Polly came out. At least I took it to be Polly. There was a small pair of feet in brown shoes moving along under a package that completely concealed the individual who was carrying it.

Back to Tongueslip and to bedmaking!

Do you think the vacuum cleaner would work? It would not. It has had periodic spells of temperament for twenty years, but I have always felt that with a little oil here and a little prod there it would carry me through another season. This time it gave up the ghost.

"Mary Katharine?"

"Yes, Mommy."

"Please go up to Mocklers' and ask Dick for a Hoover, will you? He'll lend me one."

Mary K. went and got the vacuum cleaner. I plugged it in. It went through the attic like a bulldozer, picking up everything from tacks to marbles, which may be why, eventually, the other one got tired out. Anyhow I liked that cleaner and said so. The Duchess suggested that we keep it. I turned this thought over in my mind while cleaning the attic. This time I could not follow my usual procedure, which is to pick up whatever happens to be in the way at the moment and dump it somewhere else. Every room and every bed in Tongueslip was bespoken. I had to clean house!

Tommy got some shellac and a brush and did the floors as I cleaned them. Mary K. took the boxes I have been intending for two years to take to Church World Service, and put them over in the parish house where they belonged. Polly tidied the drawers of the third-floor dressers and made room in the top two by the simple expedient of throwing away everything that was in them. It was just as well. I have not the slightest idea what was there, and if we ever had wanted it, I couldn't have found it. Except for the half yard of bed ticking which I wanted immediately to patch the pillow I had opened for the owls in 1948, but which like the rest was " gone with the wind."

By dinnertime Tongueslip was unrecognizable. The front door was washed. The third floor was shellacked. The kitchen courtyard was piled high with stuffed animals losing their stuffings, tin trains with no wheels, magazines which probably had something I had intended to read in 1942 and hadn't gotten around to, odd glassware and pitchers with broken handles which I was going to mend sometime, scraps of cretonne and every other gadjabbit that I had procrastinated upon since the last migration hit this area.

For the first time in years I had gotten around to buying sheets and towels instead of thinking, I'll do it next week. The silver was polished, the hot-water heater worked, we had a new vacuum cleaner, Tommy had mended the wallpaper on the stairs, and the nostalgic note of the first white-throated sparrow, singing his evening vesper from the pine tree, found

the inhabitants of Tongueslip in perfect and presentable array
to welcome with open arms, warm affection, and real enthusiasm the migratory human beings who have made it their
stopping place.

[28]

HOWEVER much one loves company, it requires a certain
amount of time to recover from such an invasion. One stays
up too late, succumbs to the charm of after-dinner coffee, uses
up a terrific charge of energy trying to see that all the eggs
are boiled for the required time, and that everybody has
towels, soap, and sufficient time to use them.

Fresh air becomes a must. One dresses in slacks and a
sweater and gets the lawn rake from the goosehouse.

Children, returning from the store, carry great orange
pumpkins in their arms. Mothers succumb to the crusty dough-
nuts at the bakery and fathers buy cider to make the treat
complete. It is still too early for jack-o'-lanterns, but who can
resist the fruits of fall?

Mary Katharine drinks some cider and as a result begins to
wheeze and cough with a bad bout of asthma.

To amuse her and keep her quiet at the same time, I drag
out the latest volume of the guest book at Tongueslip.

Now I'm sorry that I didn't go over it myself much earlier
in the game. But she is interested to hear about Zingling
Chan, the Confucian, who visited us quite regularly when the
Duchess was in the importing business, and about Johnny
Calicut, who was a confirmed Buddhist, and about some of
our Moslem friends. This, of course, led to *The National Geo-
graphic Magazine*. I told her what the warehouse man in New
York once told me about that. He said that there were more

National G's in storage warehouses than any other single item. No one can ever bear to throw them away. In this respect at least we follow the social pattern. We have them all, from time immemorial.

Mary K. and I turned the pages, looking at the pictures, and I determined again that someday I would write the Society and ask that they *please* put the pictures vertically on the pages. In bound volumes it is so hard to turn the book around and talk about the beautiful photos to the kids.

We came to the pictures of lighthouses, and, of course, the Cape May light. This tall white shaft, with its maroon top, is a mecca for ornithologists. It stands overlooking Brandywine Shoals, out across Delaware Bay and to the wide Atlantic.

In the early fall, when the osprey makes her flight, Cape May Point is the take-off spot for most of the land birds of northeastern America, and a resting point for thousands of shore birds.

Robert's sister, Sarah, to whom you have not yet been properly introduced for the very simple reason that she does not live at Tongueslip, is, like the rest of us, a confirmed naturalist. One year Sarah had the best of her many strokes of genius concerning my birthday.

" Why not let's take Mary to Cape May for a present. That would be something she would really love."

How right Sally was!

So Sally, Robert, Tommy, Sally's son Bob, and I set off. We planned to meet Mac and d'Arcy there — and, I'm afraid, to pick d'Arcy's brains for a knowledge of the many rare and wondrous birds that I was quite incapable of identifying for myself.

We arrived late at night and found our way to Mrs. Shaffer's house, which is right on the ocean. She specializes in birders and serves them an early and hearty breakfast. But we did not wait for morning to bird. A south wind was blowing and backing the migrants up along the shore.

The white shaft of light from the beacon swung through the starlit dark, and in its revealing rays we could see Aluco's tribe, the barn owls, in flocks soaring and circling, trying to decide whether or not to attempt the crossing.

Night herons "wooked" deeply, calling to each other in a caucus of contradictory arguments concerning the safety of the journey into a head wind. The moon rose in full splendor out of the ocean, and the dark silhouette of great blue herons streamed across its ruddy face. I would have given much if the other children could have shared that sight, but we felt that for Margaret, Sally's daughter, Mary K., and Polly the trip was too long. Malcolm and his wife, Martha Ann, were then living in Kentucky with their small fry, and for them the journey was out of the question too. We laughed and hoped that they would see Aluco's friends, the herons, and the rest, at the other end of the trip. They constantly held the Audubon Sanctuary out as bait for us.

For a while the night was still, and then close at hand the silver sleigh bells of Hyla Crucifer, the tree toad, rang out.

Robert turned the beam of his flashlight on an ancient oak under which we were standing. Tiny Hyla's eyes glowed back at us and he was silent. When the light was removed from his hiding place, his throat swelled again, and the jingling of thousands of bells joined his from the trees and shrubbery.

In the early morning we put on our bathing suits and ran across the beach into the surf. It was cold, and to keep afloat we had to strike out between the crests of the combers. I was glad that Robert and d'Arcy are strong swimmers, for I had a moment of doubt as to my ability to cope with the current. We swam far out and coasted in on the white manes of the waves.

The cold, clear water, the tang of frost in the air, the hard sand underfoot, filled me with a sense of utter aliveness that I have never had before or since. I felt an indescribable well-being, an awareness of every tingling nerve, a hypersensitivity

223

to life and everything about us that was proclaiming the surging plan of creation.

Tommy and young Bob ran across the white beach where the paw prints of Lotor the racoon and the tiny tracks of field mice marked a trail from the remains of a great striper. Beyond the breakwater there were flocks of sea birds wheeling and calling, seeking snappers and perch.

Dressed against the whistling wind, we went to sit on the strong wooden bulwark. The gulls and terns were patrolling the tide rip, and each time one seized a fish the parasitic jaegers would swoop down and steal the prize.

Redheaded ducks, goldeneyes, and scaup rode the waves in huge rafts, and across the horizon scoters and cormorants streamed in clouds.

We walked up the beach among the fragrant bayberries and the beach plums. The shrubs were alive with warblers waiting for a favorable wind. Myrtles, with their golden rumps; Cape Mays, with the tiny initialed c on their cheeks; black-throated blues, the loveliest of all; bay-breasted; and a host of other creatures flitted from twig to twig like drifting leaves of every hue.

Back along the Avalon Causeway, the plovers strolled leisurely along the mud flats, black-bellied; and by a miracle a belated golden, still in his shining breeding plumage.

Dowitchers stitched their way along the shore, like animated sewing machines, bills driving up and down into the muck, seeking food for their flight.

Robert strolled leisurely toward a small tree and reached up into its branches. Bob and Tommy clambered up and threw down the fruit. We joined them and feasted on the pungent wild persimmons before starting across the dunes.

These huge sand hills have stood watch along the shore since time immemorial, and the gnarled old hollies laden with scarlet berries hold the land with their roots against the encroaching sea and wind.

224

Here in a sheltered spot we watched a red-breasted nut-hatch click his way head downward on a stark dead tree, while overhead the hawks circled in kettles, trying to catch a warm updraft that would drift them lazily across the wide expanse of water.

A gun banged in the distance and we saw two gunners dropping the majestic hawks into the water where they could not possibly be retrieved. These too are always with us, but they were shooting legally — if wantonly — and the law, such as it is, is the law.

We tried not to hear the crying of the wounded birds struggling in the water, but it was unescapable. I could see the line of Mac's jaw tighten. She has always been a champion of mercy. Kindness is her creed.

Across the fields near the lake was a stricken giant of the forest, and working methodically up its trunk was a great spot of scarlet. We turned our glasses on it. A redheaded woodpecker was busily engaged in spearing grubs from the rotted wood. One would think that a woodpecker would get a dreadful headache banging like a jackhammer all day, but he seems to enjoy it.

We wandered toward the house, dimly aware of a pleasant hunger. Everyone was standing by the back door staring at a bush. We stood quite still until signaled to come in, and then we too watched.

Sitting on the topmost branch, alone in his glory, was a bird about the size of a sparrow with a golden-yellow breast, a small black bib, and a throat vibrating with song.

The dickcissel! None of us had ever seen him before. He left the East and retreated to the plains before I was born, but now he is making a comeback and sometimes, with luck such as we had that day, this " miniature lark " raises his canticle for the delight of birders.

Silence, a lift of wings, and he was gone, but the mocking bird picked up his refrain, whistled again like a cardinal, aped the chickadee, and then, as though he felt that the time had come for evensong, rippled into the chiming notes of the hermit thrush, and was still.

[29]

THE north wind is whistling down from the tundra, and across the blue sky of autumn the wedges of honkers come trumpeting along the ridge.

The wild goose weather vane turns to greet them and the scarlet leaves of the Virginia creeper drift through the air as though longing to join their flight.

The first thin slivers of ice hang on the sides of the fishpond, seeking to reach toward each other and seal the covenant of winter.

Salar the Salmon has gone down to the sea, and the golden plover is beating his way across the wide Pacific. The seeds of the mountain laurel lie dormant in the soil, and the lemming is curled in a snug ball beneath the arctic snow.

Tom and Mary K. and Polly, with their mittens clamped in their teeth, are working along the nets, banding the snowbirds which are coming through in hundreds. Soon the kinglets will arrive, and Robert and I will hold them in our hands and blow the crown feathers gently to see the drops of ruby and gold on their tiny crests.

Tom has finished banding and is calling us to help put the garden furniture in the loft against the mischief of Halloween. This year the goblins ride on Saturday, and will be out in full force. We chuckle as we put the things in the loft, remembering the day in summer when we actually vacuumed the barn, and when just as we had finished a violent storm arose.

A crash of thunder told us of a close hit, and I shouted at the lightning: " Don't you dare hit that barn. I just cleaned it! "

Chloe looked at me. "Miss Mary, you should know better. Don't be telling the Lord his business." Sound advice as always!

Chloe is now housekeeper for Tongueslip's first tenant, where there are not so many to do for and where a much-traveling family leaves her with long periods of richly deserved leisure. Laura is with us now at Tongueslip, and I wonder daily what we have ever done to deserve such love, such loyalty, such affection, from those whose selfless hands have been of paramount importance to Tongueslip, and whose presence, holding the ends together, has been a pivot upon which whatever use we may have been in the community has turned.

A gush of air out of the northeast sends the weather vane spinning, and white flakes settle on the back of the old gander.

The voices of the children rise in shrill excitement: "Little snow, big snow! Big snow, little snow! It's going to lie — look at it on the bird feeders!"

Downy woodpeckers, nuthatches, jays, swoop down for food before the white blanket makes foraging difficult, and Bandit, the raccoon, pokes his black nose questioningly from his house, sniffs the air, and retreats into his hollow log to sleep until the day is warmer.

Slowly the crystal flakes drift down and I turn to Robert. "How I wish I could ice a cake as smoothly as the Lord ices the world!"

"I think, darlin', that when you have been at it as long, you can!"

The Duchess looks out the window, her slender hand holding the draw cords of the curtain. Tom offers a penny for her thoughts.

"I was thinking of the last time I drove in a sleigh through a snowstorm — it was so long ago, yet only yesterday."

She hears again the jingle of silver sleigh bells and the crisp sound of a cutter, skimming behind a pair of bays, up to the top of the mountain and through the park.

Grandmother Arny recalls the days of homesteading in Washington Territory, and is immediately surrounded by Tom, Mary K., Polly, and Suzie, Lulu, and Johnny Love. They hang breathless on her tale of the day she was riding her pony through the snow and came upon a bobcat.

From the window I watch as the setting sun breaks through the storm clouds. It is an early winter and many of the leaves are still on the trees. The scarlets, and golds against the white carpet, the last of the zinnias and marigolds, the triumphant chrysanthemums bowed under the weight of ermine capes, proclaim in eternal triumph the crowning of the year.

Allhallows Eve, filled with remembered things!

The evening star burns clear. Children call to each other as they make their way down the street with bobbing jack-o'-lanterns. The ghosts and goblins walk, as in the dim and misty past when the Druids held their festival and built bonfires in honor of the sun-god, thanksgiving for harvest, and when Saman, Lord of Death, summoned the evil souls to earth for an accounting.

On this same night Pomona's feast, sung of by Ovid, was celebrated in ancient Rome with nuts and fruits and apples and now, as the vigil of Hallowmas, the eve of All Saints' Day, it is celebrated throughout Christendom. So we are still twined with the ancient gods. The years roll on.

On one Allhallows Eve a man sat at a desk, the goose quill in his hand dipped in ink made from the fluid of a squid. The pen moved quickly: "Number ninety-five" — on Allhallows Eve four centuries ago.

And in the morning that same hand drove nails into a certain door. The door of All Saint's Church, in Wittenberg, on All Saints' Day.

November 1, 1517, the radio had not been invented, but had it been, it would have shouted, "Martin Luther has defied the established Church and has nailed ninety-five theses to the door of the Church of All Saints in Wittenberg."

Shortly thereafter programs would have been periodically interrupted to scream, "Martin Luther — heretic — declared outlaw — free to be hunted — seized — done to death — wanted, dead or alive!" But they never caught him.

Four hundred and thirty-six years later, because he had never recanted, because he had said, "I will tell you what I think: I have the right to believe freely, to be a slave to no man's authority, to confess only what appears to me to be true," the church bells of Christendom pealed forth the stately notes of "A Mighty Fortress Is Our God," and in Montclair hundreds of people from every walk of life streamed toward the Central Presbyterian Church to celebrate the interdenominational service in commemoration of Luther's stand.

Central Presbyterian is a beautiful church, red-brick colonial, and the interior is perfectly adapted for such a service. The wide galleries surrounding it, the pure white pews, the spacious nave, will seat one thousand people and there were standees. I stood at the door of the sanctuary, helping to line up the choirs.

The small fry from the junior groups stood trying not to whisper. Hymnbooks in hand, white surplices freshly starched, hair brushed till it shone, faces gleaming from scrubbing, two hundred children, Negro, white, Chinese, Congregational, Methodist, Presbyterian, Episcopalian, Reformed, Evangelical, Baptist, and Collegiate, left foot forward, with a deep breath, they started down the aisle.

The rising of hundreds, the turning of the leaves of their hymnals, made a sound like the roaring of the wind across wide waters.

Then came the high school choirs, followed by the seniors: white vestments, scarlet robes, blue vestments, sober black, three hundred men and women of all races, all denominations, all ages.

The organ rolled into a fanfare between the stanzas.

Then came the clergy, some old and bent, leaning on the arms of their brothers, some young and wide-eyed, some in the prime of life, some with a touch of gray at their temples.

From the door I could see them streaming toward the galleries and the choir stalls and the altar:

Polly, with her eyes intent on the book, struggling to read the long and not too familiar words; Mary Katharine, eyes up and shouting them out from memory; Tom, walking now so like a man, deliberate, poised, controlled; Robert shortening his long strides, his baritone blending in perfect harmony with the basso profundo of the Negro man behind him; the choir of Chloe's church, with the deep rich eighth notes I have always envied.

I looked over the congregation: the Duchess and Grandmother Arny standing on tiptoe, singing fit to burst, and the clergy as they passed me, nodding, not to me, but to the parson of Tongueslip whom they, as I, sensed standing behind me.

And suddenly I felt my left foot tapping — even a Hottentot could not have remained unmoved — and I heard my own voice joining in the chorus, and Aunt Mary's, and Father Arny's, and Unkie's, and Aunty Fern's, and all the others who have sung, and danced, and loved, and laughed at Tongueslip — Catholic, Moslem, Protestant, Confucian, Buddhist, Jew, agnostic — surely, surely, all could join wholeheartedly in this!

> " Forward through the ages,
> In unbroken line,
> Move the faithful spirits
> At the call divine:
> Gifts in diff'ring measure,
> Hearts with one accord,
> Manifold the service,
> One the sure reward." [1]

[1] Frederick L. Hosmer. Copyright by The Beacon Press, Inc. Used by permission.